Experiential Astrology

symbolic journeys using guided imagery

Babs Kirby

THE CROSSING PRESS
FREEDOM, CALIFORNIA

For information on bulk purchases or group discounts for this and other Crossing Press titles, please contact our Special Sales Manager at 800-777-1048.

Visit our Web site on the Internet: www.crossingpress.com

Set in Minion 11/16.

Library of Congress Cataloging-in-Publication Data

Kirby, Babs.
    Experiential astrology : symbolic journeys using guided imagery / Babs Kirby.
       p. cm.
    Includes bibliographical references.
    ISBN 0-89594-798-6 (pbk.)
    1. Astrology. 2. Imagery (Psychology)--Therapeutic use. 3. Self-actualization (Psychology)--Miscellanea--Problems, exercises, etc. I. Title.
BF1729.S38K57 1997
133.5--dc21   97-26023
                                         CIP

To my Mum and Dad,
Doreen and Harry Fitch

I would like to thank all those who have helped me, both directly and indirectly, in writing this book. First, I must thank those who have allowed me to include their journeys and charts in these pages: Ann, Elise, Jill, Joe, Lance, Michael, Olivia, and Rory. Though I use pseudonyms here to protect identities, you know who you are, and I am extremely grateful to you all. I am also grateful to all who have ever taken these journeys with me; you have encouraged and supported me in this work, and without you this book would never have been written.

The chapters on Mercury, Venus, and Mars draw from work Janey Stubbs and I did together. The chapter on Mercury contains material adapted from one of our workshops. The chapters on Venus and Mars benefit from our collaboration on the book *Love and Sexuality: An Exploration of Venus and Mars*, published by Element Books.

I am grateful to those who have read and commented on the manuscript as it progressed. My editors at The Crossing Press, Linda Gunnarson and Judith Pynn, have helped focus my thinking, and have been generally supportive. Sue Tompkins gave constructive feedback on the Mercury chapter. Sandra Levy has been wonderfully encouraging and has given invaluable feedback on each chapter of the manuscript. Aleathea Lillitos has been a generous and supportive friend. Aleathea has made useful comments on the manuscript throughout and offered her insight into the participants' guided imagery journeys, which I have incorporated into my commentaries. I would also like to thank Ananda Bagley at Electric Ephemeris for producing the birth charts and for being so obliging.

Finally, I would like to acknowledge all those I have trained with or worked alongside, who have helped me on my journey. In particular, I thank my friends and colleagues at the Faculty of Astrological Studies, Barbara Somers and the late Ian Gordon Brown at The Center for

Transpersonal Psychology, and Marianne Jacoby, whose Jungian perspective has percolated through and to all those who have influenced me during my years of involvement in humanistic psychology.

This is the book I always wanted to write. I am grateful to the late John Gill of The Crossing Press for making it possible. As we go to press, Saturn opposes my Neptune; the dream becomes a reality.

Contents

Introduction

This book emerges out of my background as a humanistic psychotherapist and an astrologer, and is a synthesis of two important strands of my personal development over the last 25 years.

I was involved in humanistic psychology first. My interest in astrology developed out of my desire to understand the human psyche. The birth chart provides a map of the psyche and its potential that does not pathologize or make judgments, a map that enables us to understand both our inner worlds and the outer manifestation of our lives. Our horoscope describes our character, offers perspective on our life patterns, and reveals the timing of inner change. The astrological perspective offers a paradigm by which we can make sense of the relationship between our character and the outer events of our lives.

In the last twenty years or so there has been a quiet but definite revolution in the way astrologers interpret charts. The shift was pioneered by astrologers like Donna Cunningham, Liz Greene, Tracy Marks, Christina Rose, Dane Rudhyar, and Howard Sasportas, to name just a few, and followed by others with a psychological background. Increasingly, astrologers are offering interpretations that acknowledge the gap between outer behavior and inner experience, recognizing that an external description has a limited value and needs to be married to an understanding of what an astrological placement actually *feels* like. Addressing a client's inner reality validates their personal experience, helps them feel understood, and can be therapeutic.

As a psychotherapist and astrologer, I was in the privileged position of hearing my psychotherapy clients speak their charts. As a consequence, I became increasingly aware of the ways in which the various planetary placements and aspects were experienced. There was a richness and diversity that I rarely found in the "cook book" interpretations of astrologers. At the same time, I taught astrology and could see the problem students had in understanding what the inner experiences of astrological placements might be. Many students are studying astrology to gain access to their own inner world and understand themselves better. I wanted to find a way of revealing a person's chart to him or her in an experiential way, a way that related directly to their inner experience.

Each planet symbolizes a drive , energy, or urge and has a core meaning that is specific to that planet. For instance, Mars represents our survival instincts, our sex drive, and our ability to assert ourselves and defend our territory. We see the planetary energies manifesting in our psyche as conscious and unconscious drives as well as in our experiences of others and the outer world. Part of the core curriculum for any student of astrology is the study of the planets and the underlying principles that each planet represents. There is a general introduction to the planets in chapter 1 and a more detailed explanation of each of the planetary principles at the beginning of chapters 2 through 11.

Humanistic psychology is rich in experiential techniques that access the inner world, so I decided to draw on one of the techniques—guided imagery—and set about writing journeys that would evoke the specific planetary principles. During a guided imagery journey, a person is able to access their own images related to a particular planetary principle, and as a consequence understands this principle in a personal way. The type of knowledge which is grounded in experience, as opposed to head-learning, is unforgettable and can be drawn on whenever needed.

While I have developed the use of guided imagery, others have explored different techniques. Prudence Jones, in her ground-breaking anthology *Creative Astrology: an Experiential Understanding of the Horoscope*, draws together in one volume the teachings and methods of pioneers of experiential astrology. My chapter in the anthology is titled "Symbols, Guided Imagery and the Person-Centered Approach." (I have developed and expanded these ideas in this book.)

Experiential Astrology: symbolic journeys using guided imagery presents ten guided imagery journeys: for the Sun, the Moon, and each of the planets. Through taking the imagery journeys, readers can experience the planetary principles for themselves in a powerful and helpful way. In each chapter, the particular planet's symbolism is discussed, and the guided imagery journey is presented. Guidelines for interpreting the journeys are included alongside accounts of the experiences of others who have been on the journeys, along with their charts. Even if you don't seek a direct experience yourself, you can still glimpse the richness of other people speaking their charts.

This book is designed as a workbook and will benefit those interested in understanding astrological symbolism in a personal way. It is ideal for use in a group, each member sharing their images with the others, the group exploring together the astrological symbolism. Each member hears the many very personal ways a single planetary principle can be experienced, and thus their astrological understanding is enriched.

Those without any prior astrological knowledge can also make use of this book, experiencing the guided imagery journeys and using the guidelines to interpret their experience. The journeys facilitate self-understanding and insight and will aid clarification of a wide spectrum of issues. It can be used whether or not the reader wishes to take up the study of astrology. For those looking for help with specific issues, recommendations in Chapter 1 guide you to an appropriate journey.

In this book I am drawing in particular on material from two series of ten workshops that I presented and on various individual sessions. I am grateful to the participants who agreed to have their journeys and their charts published, and while I have changed names, and excluded birth data to protect their anonymity, all else has remained unaltered. These guided imagery journeys were presented in a ten-day Astrodrama Course in Greece and are part of the personal growth component of the Faculty of Astrological Studies' *Counseling within Astrology* two-year course. They have also been used in many single workshops, and while nothing is published from these sources, I am nevertheless drawing on all my experience. This work has given me great pleasure, and I hope those reading this book will share it.

CHAPTER 1

Introduction to
Guided Imagery

☉ ☽ ☿ ♀ ♂ ♃ ♄ ♅ ♆ ♇

Experiential astrology is a relatively new concept and is to astrology what the innovative new therapies that sprung up in the '60s and '70s under the humanistic psychology banner are to psychoanalysis. The new therapies have matured and been modified over the years. Humanistic practitioners have learned through experience that some of the traditional ideas were useful after all, and have incorporated these ideas into their practice. What humanistic psychology lacked in clear boundaries, it made up for in its eagerness to explore new frontiers and to challenge more orthodox analytical approaches. The cross-fertilization went both ways; many of the concepts in the new therapies have now been taken on board by the more orthodox therapies, broadening and enlivening them, and breaking down some of the analytic rigidity. Similarly, astrology will be modified and changed by emerging innovative approaches while being confirmed in its basic principles.

Experiential astrology is a way to experience astrology directly, without an interpreter. It is a way to perceive your own relationship to the planetary principles. I focus in this book on guided imagery, but other practitioners are adapting techniques from the newer therapies. Drama therapy, psychodrama, and Gestalt therapy all combine easily with astrology, providing a direct experience to participants.

Gestalt therapy, an innovation of Fritz Perls, has its roots in existential-ism. Gestalt is famous for its "chairwork," where an individual moves from one chair to another as they embody and identify with the two sides of a conflict. Gestalt lends itself to astrology in that it promotes the idea of dialogue between conflicting parts of the psyche. Conflict, experienced as inner or outer, can be shown astrologically by planets in challenging aspect to each other. Astrologers are using the ideas inherent in Gestalt psychotherapy to dialogue between the drives represented by the planets' placements. For example, if a person has a Venus Uranus square, they may identify with the part of themselves that wants closeness, relatedness, love, and companionship, and project out onto another the part of themselves that wants space, freedom, autonomy, and independence. Connecting to the internal conflict through Gestalt chairwork both illuminates and helps to dissolve the split.

Psychodrama, developed by Jacob Moreno, draws on members of a group to enact a scenario that relates to one of the group. Psychodrama has well-established rules, including the idea of a protagonist (whose scene is enacted) and a director, the group facilitator. Astrodrama has adapted this technique. A group can act out the whole chart of one of its members with other members taking on the roles of the different planets in their respective signs and houses. The dialogue that ensues between actors can reveal very real inner dilemmas to the protagonist.

Dramatherapy incorporates props, such as make-up, masks and costumes, and many of those working in astrodrama have included the methods of dramatherapy in their work. Friedel Roggenbuck asks each group member to play a part of themselves, enacting a particular planet in their own chart. There is no script. Part of getting into the role is the whole ritual of putting on make-up and selecting a costume. Once in touch with their role, group members spend time making contact with others in the group, who are each in their own different roles. This allows participants to see how an aspect of themselves operates in many different situations. The work can be emotionally powerful and illuminating.

In this book, guided imagery is our method. The roots of guided imagery go back over two and a half thousand years. It was used in the Aesclepian temples of Greece, and has survived in some form or another to this day. Guided imagery, guided meditations, and visualizations are used by healers and by several branches of psychotherapy. My use is just one of many.

Assagioli used visualization extensively and developed its use in the psychospiritual branch of psychotherapy known as Psychosynthesis. Transpersonal Psychology employs imaging techniques extensively. I have learned much from the way Ian Gordon Brown and Barbara Somers work with spot imaging, guided imagery, and the guided day dream. Jung used active imagination, and had specific rules about its use. He believed it was wrong to use images of people known to us and in my use of guided imagery journeys I have heeded this. I ask participants to imagine only imaginary people, not people they know.

Those working in the shamanistic traditions throughout the ages also use visualizations. A man working in the Native American traditions first told me that in imaging work, participants must be taken back to the place from which they started their journey. This is something else I have heeded. Imagery is used in various ways in many branches of healing, and is one of the most accepted alternative techniques. I have employed guided imagery to explore a more personal experience of astrology.

Many who come to study astrology do so for self-knowledge. It is a way to understand life and is the beginning, for many, of an important phase of personal growth. We begin to look at ourselves and our lives from a different perspective, an astrological perspective, which means we begin to understand our inner character and its relationship to the phases of change and growth in our life in a new way.

These times of change are described by our transits, the passages of the planets in the sky over the planets in our birth chart, and by progressions, a symbolic way of moving the planets forward that correlates with how life unfolds for each of us. The planets represent various drives within us.

Transits and progressions set off these drives, bringing aspects of ourselves into greater consciousness. Our experience of a transit or progression will vary, depending on how able we are to express the planetary principle concerned. The less able we are to recognize a planetary principle or drive as our own, the more likely it is to manifest as an external event in our life. If we are not in touch with ourselves, our lives can appear to be at the mercy of fate. This is the way our character creates our fate; if our fate does not please us, it can be helpful to get a better understanding of our character.

We can work with our transits and progressions in a retrospective way, looking at the important past events of our lives and mapping the transits and progressions that were occurring. This gives us clues to our relationship with the various planetary principles and helps prepare us to meet future transits. For instance, if we had a Saturn transit to Mars and found ourselves in an extremely frustrating situation, we can plan how to direct our Mars energy constructively when we see our next Saturn transit to Mars coming up. We know from past experience that we have a problem with Mars energy, and our current transit will illustrate for us what progress we have made with regard to this principle.

This is an intellectual and strategic way of using astrology that will help us in understanding ourselves from a detached perspective, but will not necessarily help to bring about personal change. I have witnessed many astrologers observing the events of their lives and commenting on their transits with very little awareness of their personal relationship to these events. While they have some intellectual understanding of the relationship, it is not grounded in any real personal awareness of what it actually means when events "happen" to us. Anyone who has been in counseling or psychotherapy will have had an opportunity to build bridges between what happens "out there" and what happens internally. This is the path to *individuation* that Jung speaks of, the way to self-realization.

Guided imagery on planetary principles is a way of translating astrological symbols into a more personal set of symbols so that we can understand what they actually mean to us. Through the guided imagery journeys in this book, we are presented with a series of closely-related symbolic scenarios which conjure up a planetary principle. We are free to imagine whatever comes into our mind. An exploration of the content of these journeys provides a way to connect to our own inner experience of astrological principles and bridges our understanding of astrological principles with our inner world.

Guided imagery is like a waking dream, and while the journeys have been written to evoke particular planetary principles, in practice they can evoke anything in the chart that resonates with the scenarios that are being presented. The content of our journeys relates to our whole psyche and therefore to the whole chart. The Saturn journey will not only evoke Saturn; any planet in aspect to Saturn may be evoked, as well as any planet in Capricorn and planets being transited by Saturn.

While I have written a different journey for each planet and each chapter addresses a different planetary principle, in practice other planetary principles are inevitably discernible in the content of the participant's journeys. This fact is acknowledged throughout the book. We are taking a waking dream that is full of very personal symbolism and showing how it is imbued with astrological symbolism. This personal understanding is irrevocable, unforgettable, because it is known to us and revealed, rather than learnt or taught, and it will leave us with a far more grounded understanding of our birth chart. When working in a group, we can discover a deeper, more personal way of understanding astrological symbolism and enrich our interpretation skills.

Just as dreams contain many levels of meaning, so participants' images will operate on several different levels. As we sleep, we may incorporate sounds around us into our dreams; for instance, an alarm clock going off can become a passing fire engine with its siren blasting. Ephemeral stimuli in the room can affect our images. Nevertheless, how these stimuli are incorporated is still personal, and our images will mainly relate to our current life circumstances and deep-seated inner issues. Images can relate to all three levels simultaneously. Participants can interpret and understand their images at whatever level they are open and ready to. Like dreams whose meanings elude us on waking—even though we can unravel and begin to understand them piece by piece—so these journeys will reveal more and more of ourselves to us over time.

Astrologers think symbolically. If, when listening to a client, we hear her speaking in terms of shoulds and oughts, we hear Saturn and can think in terms of Saturn's symbolism as we listen. We are able to think laterally and to speculate that this client has a strong inner critic and may be critical of herself as well as judgmental of others. If we are Freudian, we may think in terms of a strong super-ego. If we are Jungian we may think in terms of the Senex archetype. As astrologers, we may also think in terms of the father principle and want to explore the actual relationship of our client to her father, which is perhaps the root of these shoulds and oughts. We may also think in terms of the client's ambitiousness, the standards she sets herself, and the extent of her self-criticism when she is unable to keep to these standards. In all of these examples, Saturnian symbols have become constellated in the astrologer's mind, and he or she can proceed in many directions, depending on the client.

Astrologers do not need to have a client's chart in order to think in this way. This thinking is automatic for anyone steeped in the symbolism of astrology. We recognize the astrological principles manifesting in the people and things around us. It is a way of ordering and understanding our universe and our process through it. Becoming fluent in this kind of symbolic thinking is what any good astrological training is about. It means being able to move from the inner to the outer, and to see the links that constellate around a particular principle.

If you choose only to read the accounts of other people's journeys and my commentaries, you will not know how it *feels* to go on a journey. The narratives of the participants' journeys are attempts to convert what have been right-brain, *felt* experiences into left-brain, rationally explainable experiences. I urge you to go on the journeys for yourself. Then the accounts and my commentaries will really come to life. The complexity and subtlety of astrological interpretation draws on the right brain, which governs the intuitive and creative aspects of the mind and facilitates a lateral way of thinking. The journeys in this book develop this creative dimension of the mind.

For Those Without Prior Astrological Knowledge

The following information is included for those who are new to astrology, to help you use this book effectively.

There are three basic building blocks that astrologers use when interpreting a chart: the planets, the signs, and the houses. Although the Sun and Moon are not planets, we bracket them together with Mercury, Venus, Mars, Jupiter, Saturn, Uranus, Neptune, and Pluto, and commonly refer to them all as planets. We see the planets as representing different drives, or principles. When we speak of planetary principles, we are referring to the principle that is associated with a particular planet. A separate chapter is dedicated to each of the planets, in which its principle is described. As an introduction, I will give some key words for each planet so that you will begin to get a feel for them. We speak of masculine and feminine principles, but it is important to differentiate these from male and female gender. We have all the planets in our chart and hence have all these principles operating within us, whatever our gender.

THE PLANETS

Sun— spirit, heart, center, authenticity, integrity, essence, core, vitality, radiance, consciousness, the father, masculine, the yang principle, life goals, priorities, background character.

Moon— soul, feelings, instincts, past, habits, responsiveness, receptivity, nurturing, the unconscious, the mother, feminine, the yin principle, everyday personality, the inner child.

Mercury— thinking, communicating, trickster, mimic, logos, logic, reasoning, mediation, physical dexterity, flexibility, movement, siblings.

Venus— love, attraction, unity, harmony, social adeptness, beauty, art, eros, feminine, yin principle, money.

Mars— sexuality, assertion, survival, force, strength, willpower, courage, determination, differences, yang, masculine principle, the person in action.

Jupiter— expansion, growth, learning, faith, confidence, generosity, buoyancy, philosophy, religion, natural laws of life, traveling.

Saturn— self-control, discipline, ambition, perseverance, seriousness, limitations, concentration, restrictions and obstacles, consensus, the rules, authority, the father.

Uranus— detachment, independence, freedom, awakening, exhilaration, impersonal, truth, sudden insight, extremes, rebellion, cold, restlessness, change.

Neptune— idealism, imagination, sensitivity, magic, mysticism, illusion, mystery, confusion, escape, receptivity, impressionability.

Pluto— power, transformation, sex, death, birth, rebirth, renewal, magic, occult, decay, destruction, stagnation, unconscious, repression.

THE SIGNS

Within a birth chart, each of the planets will fall in one of the signs of the zodiac: Aries, Taurus, Gemini, Cancer, Leo, Virgo, Libra, Scorpio, Sagittarius, Capricorn, Aquarius, or Pisces, which will color and modify the way in which the planet is expressed. The signs are the second of the basic building blocks that astrologers use, and most of you will have some knowledge of the signs. This is linked with what we call sun sign or star sign astrology, and a little lateral thinking is needed when trying to understand how the Moon or Mercury might express itself in the various signs. With the help of this book, you can go on a guided imagery journey which will give you a direct experience of how you express any given planet in the sign it falls in in your birth chart. You can go on to read the journeys of others, to see how their journeys have varied depending on the sign the planet is placed in.

THE HOUSES

The third building block we call the houses. These are the segments into which a birth chart is divided, which begin with the rising sign or the Ascendant. The Ascendant is based on the time of birth. The earth rotates on its axis once every 24 hours, a day and a night. During this 24-hour period, each of the signs of the zodiac is on the horizon for a period of time, and the sign on the horizon is what is known as your rising sign, or Ascendant. When an astrologer calculates your chart, she calculates the exact degrees and minutes of your Ascendant, based on the time of birth and the latitude and longitude of the place where you were born. Most astrologers use computers to do this nowadays. In the appendix some computer calculation services are listed for those who do not have their own chart and would like to get it calculated.

The houses in a birth chart are counted from the Ascendant, which is always the start of the first house. We call the beginning of a house the "cusp." There are various ways that astrologers divide the chart up and obtain the house cusps. I use the placidus house system, which divides the 24-hour period of the earth's rotation into 12 equal segments and takes as the various house cusps the degree that would be rising every two hours. The technicalities need not concern you, unless you have a strong curiosity, but you do need to know something of the meaning of the different houses.

We number the houses from the Ascendant in a counterclockwise direction, and each house describes an area of life and of experience. Just as the Ascendant is the cusp of the first house, the Descendant, the point opposite, is the cusp of the seventh house. The MC and IC are the cusps of the tenth and fourth houses, respectively. These are especially sensitive points within the natal chart.

First House— physical appearance, self image, physical body, outer personality, how one meets and interacts with the environment, approach to life.

Second House— personal resources, earning power, values, attitudes to money and financial security, emotional sufficiency, physical assets.

Third House— local environment, neighbors, siblings, communication (letters, telephone, newspapers, television, and radio), school, mental interests, short journeys.

Fourth House— inner self, private life, home, domestic situation, past, ancestral roots, parents, family, land, end of life, psychological conditioning.

Fifth House— self-expression, identity, creativity, play, fun, children, leisure, speculation and gambling, sport, entertainment, artistic pursuits, romance and love affairs.

Sixth House— service, daily routines, duties, efficiency, work, health, sickness, diet, hygiene, mind/body relationship, employer/employee relationships, pets.

Seventh House— others, the public, marriage, one-to-one relationships, partnerships, open enemies, divorce, contracts, conflicts, joint actions, cooperation.

Eighth House— sex, shared feelings, deep involvement with others, shared possessions and money, tax, insurance, inheritance, legacies, the occult, transformation, birth, death.

Ninth House— meaning and purpose of life, mind-expanding experiences, long distance travel, study, law, philosophy, religion, foreign matters, publishing, broadcasting, prophecy, in-laws.

Tenth House— status, reputation, public image, career, profession, goals, ambition, social contribution and standing, achievements, the boss, parents.

Eleventh House— aspirations, ideals, hopes and wishes, broad objectives, transpersonal motivation, social circle, friends, peer groups, societies.

Twelfth House— inner life, solitude, contemplation, reverie, introspection, mysticism, secrets, sacrifice, repression, secret enemies, hidden strengths and weaknesses, prisons, hospitals, psychiatric units, places of retreat.

It takes considerable skill and experience to interpret a planet in a sign and in a house. A metaphor that may be helpful is to see the birth chart as a play, with each planet an actor. The sign it is in is the script, and the house is the scenery. When you go on the journeys, you will see that the house a planet is in will manifest in the scenery of your journey.

THE ASPECTS

Astrologers also talk about aspects. We say a planet is in aspect to another planet when it is a certain number of degrees away, and depending on the number of degrees, the aspect will have a different name and meaning. The main aspects referred to in this book are:

Conjunction— when planets are within 8 degrees of each other, they literally are conjoined and work in unity. This creates a particular strength and emphasis.

Opposition— when planets are about 180 degrees apart (we allow between 172 and 188 degrees), they literally oppose each other across the chart and create a polarity within the psyche. This enhances awareness and difference, gives objectivity, and produces tension.

Square— when planets are about 90 degrees apart (we allow between 82 and 98 degrees), they create a challenge to each other, producing struggle and tension within an individual. Often there will be concrete, external manifestations of this struggle.

Trine— when planets are about 120 degrees apart (we allow between 112 and 128 degrees), they produce a flow and are in harmony, creating ease, joy, and motivation.

Sextile— when planets are about 60 degrees apart (we allow between 56 and 64 degrees), there is an opportunity for them to work well together, but effort is required.

Semisquare— when planets are about 45 degrees apart (we allow between 43 and 47 degrees), they irritate and frustrate each other, often producing tangible achievements.

Sesquiquadrate— when planets are about 135 degrees apart (we allow between 133 and 137 degrees), they create stress and often show where a great effort is made creating tangible achievement.

Quincunx or Inconjunct— when planets are about 150 degrees apart (we allow between 148 and 152 degrees), they are at odds and uncomfortable with each other; there is strain and "dis-ease." It is difficult to come to grips with whatever the problem is, and hence, it is difficult to remedy it.

In the following chapters the texts of participants' journeys are reproduced. Where I "hear" them speaking a particular aspect in their chart, I have inserted the aspect in brackets, stating which planets are involved. This is included for those who are already astrologers and for those who want to understand astrology and how aspects can be experienced. If this is not your intention, then these asides can simply be ignored.

When to Go on Guided Imagery Journeys

The guided imagery journeys can be taken as a sequence, working through the whole book over a period of weeks or months. They can be taken in any order that appeals to you. It is important to allow sufficient time between each guided imagery journey. The images that arise when going on a journey set off unconscious processes that need time to wend their way to conscious awareness. Subsequent dreams may pick up and elaborate on some of the images invoked, so at least one night's sleep between journeys is needed. A gap of at least a week will allow the unconscious some space to process the images. I have worked with groups intensively with a daily interval but usually aim for weekly, fortnightly, or monthly intervals, all of which give a more comfortable lapse of time.

For those who have an astrological understanding, it can be helpful to go on the journey of a planet that is currently being transited. A new and deeper understanding of all that this planetary principle represents in your life is wending its way to consciousness right now—its symbolism is likely to be evident in many strands of your life—and going on the guided imagery journey can help clarify for you some of your current dilemmas.

For those without prior astrological knowledge, I recommend which journeys to go on, depending on what is currently of concern to you. If you take one journey and it has not helped clarify or illuminate your current situation, then wait a couple of days. A process has been started in your unconscious mind, and your dreams may also shed light. If this still fails to be helpful, then try a different recommended journey.

The Sun— If you are feeling uncentered or ungrounded, if you want to get a clearer sense of your identity, or if you have an important decision to make, then go on the Sun journey. The Sun journey helps you to connect to your essence, your core, and will help you to know what really matters to you.

The Moon— The Moon journey is useful when there are emotional problems within a relationship, or if you want to get in touch with a sense of where you belong, of where "home" is, both literally and metaphorically, and of how to fit in with others and life in general. The Moon is the seat of your emotional well-being, so when there is emotional turbulence in your life, the Moon journey can connect you to what the deeper, underlying emotional issues are for you.

Mercury— If you are someone who doesn't feel heard or understood, or finds it difficult to communicate what you think and believe, or if you would simply like to get a feel for your style of communicating, then try the Mercury journey. At any stage where there are communication issues or misunderstandings with friends or colleagues that have to do with "crossed wires," this journey can be helpful.

Venus— The Venus journey will help clarify issues around sexual relationships as well as help you to understand your love nature. This journey will help to put you in touch with your sensuality and clarify what your needs are within a relationship. It will also help in artistic matters and is recommended as an alternative journey to the **Sun** if you are experiencing a creative block.

Mars— This journey is of benefit when there are issues in a sexual relationship that are specifically sexual. The Mars journey helps you to get in touch with your assertiveness, independence, free will, and the way you do things. It is recommended as an alternative journey to try when decisions are called for, particularly if a situation has not been clarified by going on the **Sun** journey.

Jupiter— If you want to tune in to your urge for freedom, your desire to extend yourself, to travel and to learn, then go on the Jupiter journey. On both this and the **Saturn** journey you get in touch with an inner wise person, whom you can draw on for counsel and wisdom.

Saturn— The Saturn journey is helpful if you want to understand more about how you deal with obstacles and difficulties in your life. It can help you get hold of what your personal limits are and, along with **Mars**, help you to set boundaries for yourself. If you have problems with those in authority, then this journey can help you understand how you create this.

Uranus— If you want to gain some perspective on your life and to get in touch with a more detached part of yourself, then go on the Uranus journey. This journey helps you to know what you think about wider, less personal issues, and gives you a global perspective on yourself and the part you play in life.

Neptune— If you want to tune in to an imaginative, creative, and idealistic part of yourself, then go on the Neptune journey. This journey will put you in touch with your highest aspirations and yearnings.

Pluto— If you want to tune in to a part of yourself that has a deep inner wisdom and instinctual knowledge, then go on the Pluto journey. If you have recently suffered a loss, or are being asked to relinquish someone or something, then this is a good journey to take as it will deepen your understanding of your current situation.

Once you have chosen which guided imagery journey you would like to go on, I suggest you take it before you read the rest of its related chapter. If you read about the planetary principle first, you begin to develop preconceived ideas about what to expect. By taking the journey first, you remain more open to the imagery, and you have your own experience of the planetary principle. After the journey, you can go on to read the rest of the chapter.

Some Guidelines Before Going on These Journeys

Before we get to the journeys themselves, I'd like to go over some practicalities. Participants usually lie down to go on a guided imagery journey, but those who have practiced yoga or meditation may prefer to sit in a cross-legged position, and others may feel more comfortable sitting in a chair. When lying still for 30 minutes or so, our body temperature drops and we may feel chilled, so I recommend using a light cover. Feeling cold (or being uncomfortable in any way) will create a distraction and can affect the content of the journey, possibly with images of snow or ice!

When sitting in a chair, have both feet placed firmly on the floor and the spine straight. It is a good idea for anyone who is prone to falling asleep to stay sitting. If, when working in a group, someone near you falls asleep and begins to snore (this actually happens quite a lot), I suggest whoever is nearest give them a gentle nudge, as their snoring will disturb everyone in the group and may influence the content of the imagery.

When imaging, it is important to accept whatever images or thoughts emerge. If you censor your images or thoughts, your imaginal flow may dry up. If you have images you do not like, then stay with them and try to adapt them, but do not deny them. This is a process of surrender to the unconscious mind in its own realm, which has its own wisdom.

And please, for those of you who already have an understanding of astrological symbolism, put aside this knowledge while you go on a journey, as you will be in danger of using too much of your rational mind and your images will be impoverished. Do not try to fathom the symbolism of the journey while experiencing it. This is something to do afterwards.

The journeys vary in length, taking between 20 and 40 minutes each. You can either have someone read the guided imagery journeys out loud to you, or you can record the journey onto a tape for yourself. The journeys should be read slowly, paying attention to the pauses I have included in brackets. These are graded as short pauses, pauses, or long pauses. A short pause might be a few seconds, with a pause being a minute or two and a long pause being as much as three or four minutes, or even longer. If these journeys are rushed, the images will be impoverished. We need time to allow our imaginations to wander. It is better to err on the slow side.

It is helpful to go on a guided imagery journey with someone else present with whom we can talk through our experience afterwards. However, I advocate that as soon as the journey is over, before speaking to anyone, you write down the journey. We begin to gain some perspective and insight into our journey through the process of writing. Writing is a way of having a dialogue with ourselves. It is also important because our memory of the contents of these journeys can quickly evaporate, like the contents of dreams that fade rapidly from memory. This is a private record, one that you may want to refer back to over time or to take to your therapist if you are in therapy. When working with another or in a group, always respect a participant's right not to reveal parts of their journey.

When leading journeys myself, I provide crayons, felt-tips, and sheets of drawing paper so that participants can illustrate some of the images from their journeys. Many people initially feel very self-conscious about drawing, but once it becomes established that this is not about producing great art, rather simply another way to understand more immediately and graphically the contents of our journeys, inhibitions disappear.

You are now ready for the journeys which follow. Before you go on each of the journeys, go through the following relaxation exercise. This exercise gives your body and mind a chance to clear and become receptive to the guided imagery journey. Bon voyage!

RELAXATION EXERCISE

— Focus on your feet. Be aware of any tension in them, and relax, let them go loose. (pause)

— Focus on your calves and knees, be aware of any tension in them, and let go of it—relax. (pause)

— Focus on your thighs and buttocks, be aware of any tension in them, and relax. Feel how heavy your legs are when you let go the tension go. (pause)

— Focus on your stomach, chest and back, be aware of any tension, and relax, let go of it.

— For those lying down: Feel your back on the ground and your whole body supported. Let yourself sink into the ground.

— For those sitting: Imagine your spine as a straight rod, supporting you.

— For those sitting in a chair: Be aware of your feet on the ground.

— For all: Let your breath become slow and steady and reach right down into your stomach. (pause)

— Focus on your shoulders, arms and hands, be aware of any tension in them, and let go of it—relax. Let your hands, arms, and shoulders go limp and floppy. Be aware of how heavy your arms are when relaxed. (pause)

— Focus on your neck and jaw, be aware of any tension in them, and let go of it—relax. Let your jaw hang loose.

— For those lying down: Your head is being supported.

— For those sitting: Allow your head to rest comfortably on the top of your spine. For all: Let the tension go in your neck—relax. (pause)

— Focus on your face, your eyes, your nose, your mouth, lips, tongue, your scalp, and relax, let go of any tension, let your whole face go loose, even floppy—relax. (pause)

Take a deep breath right down into your stomach, exhaling completely and pausing before taking the next new breath. Repeat and let go of any remaining tensions in your body, and let your mind become clear, too. Let any thoughts drift by like puffs of cloud in a blue sky on a summer's day. (long pause)

The Charts

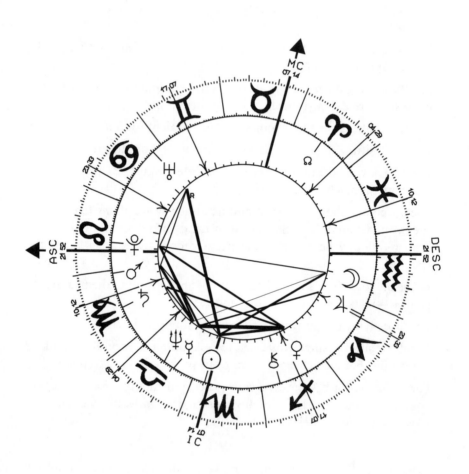

ANN'S CHART

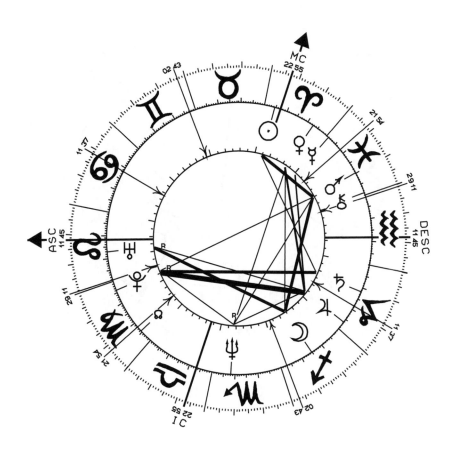

ELISE'S CHART

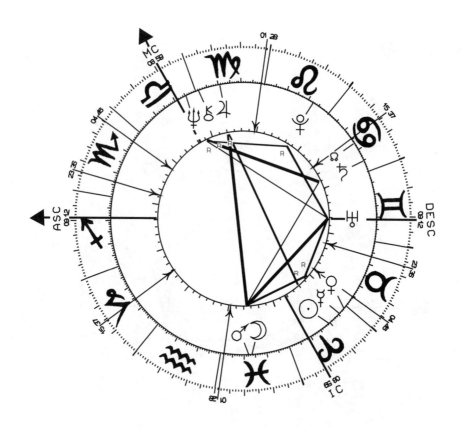

JILL'S CHART

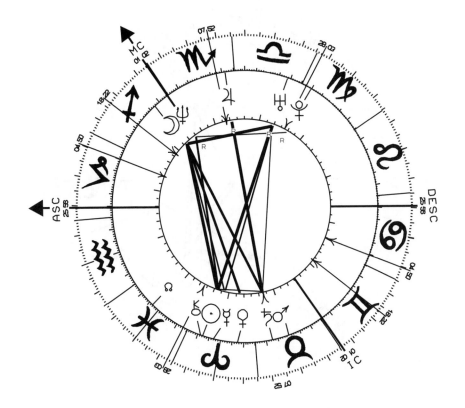

JOE'S CHART

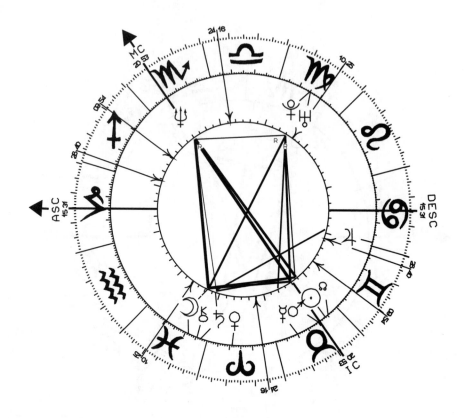

LANCE'S CHART

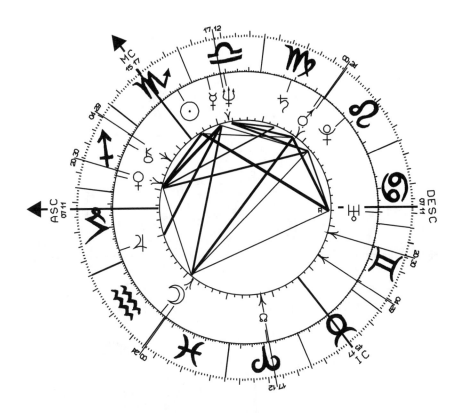

MICHAEL'S CHART

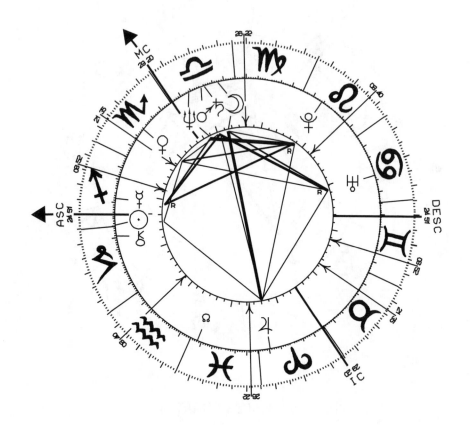

OLIVIA'S CHART

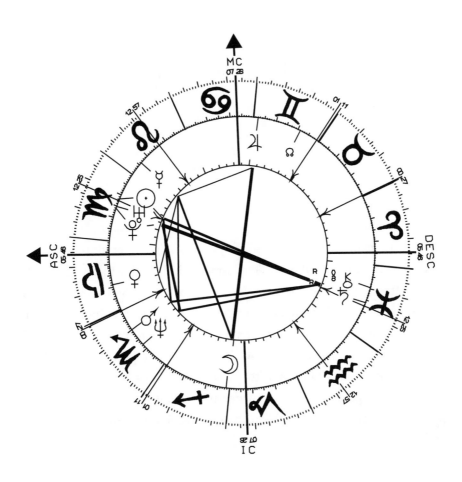

RORY'S CHART

CHAPTER 2

The Sun

The Sun is the center of our solar system. All life on earth is dependent upon it for light and heat. This astronomical fact is a metaphor for the Sun's astrological, symbolic meaning. Within us, the Sun represents our center, our heart. When we are whole-hearted about something, we are in touch with the solar principle. Our ability to be and feel authentic depends on this solar principle; if we are not in touch with it within, we may feel a fraud, we may lack vitality, and the meaning and purpose of our life may elude us. The guided imagery journey that follows can have the effect of putting us back in touch with our vitality, leaving us with renewed vigor and a sense of purpose.

The Sun symbolizes our core, our essence. More than anything the Sun journey is about contacting this essence at the utmost center of our being, which guides us not only to follow the dictates of our heart, but of our higher aspirations, our spiritual self. Going on this journey will have the effect of centering us and putting us in touch with our authentic core. If we are easily knocked off center, we will particularly benefit from using this journey, as we can recall parts of our imagery any time we need help in centering ourselves.

The Sun journey helps to put in perspective the issues currently going on in our lives, giving us an opportunity to know, from the core of our being, what really matters to us. When we are in touch with our essence, our core, then decisions are easily made; it is when we don't know who we really are that we don't know what we want and what is right for us.

Those who express the solar principle emanate a certainty. They come across as genuine, so others have confidence in them and trust them. They are seen as persons "of integrity." This certainty and confidence is not to be equated with exuberance or ostentation; it can be found in those who are quiet and self-contained. It is simply a knowing of oneself. When we lose touch with our Sun, we are adrift, and do not know who we really are, so clearly we can not inspire others to have confidence in us.

The Sun, at the center of our solar system, has all the planets revolving around it, and this, too, acts as a metaphor for us as individuals. The Sun represents the central organizing force within us, integrating the drives represented by the other planets. Another metaphor is that of an orchestra; the Sun is the conductor and the planets the various instruments. Without the conductor, there is a cacophony of noise; it is the conductor who interprets how a piece of music should be played and gives instructions to the various instrumentalists. Likewise, the Sun integrates the various drives of the planets into a synthesized whole. Without the Sun's unifying principle we become fragmented, we lose a sense of our wholeness and completeness.

Because of the sense of nobility and integrity emanating from someone who is connected with their essential self, or actively seeking it, the Sun also symbolizes the hero, who comes in many guises. In this journey we may touch on this aspect of the Sun's symbolism and see something of the hero within us.

Before you go on the Sun journey, please read the section "Some Guidelines Before Going on These Journeys" in Chapter 1 and go through the Relaxation Exercise given there.

Guided Imagery Journey on the Sun's Principle

— I want you to imagine that you are setting out on a quest. (short pause)

— You are setting out along a path or road. The Sun is overhead and you are on your way. Be aware of what the path or road is like—be aware of your surroundings. (pause)

— What is your step or pace like? (short pause)

— As you continue on your way, you see a mountain (short pause) and you walk towards it. (short pause)

— You are going to climb it. Be aware of how high it is, how easy or difficult to climb. (short pause)

— As you begin your climb, feel your feet on the ground. Experience every part of the ascent, stage by stage. (long pause)

— You have now reached the top of the mountain. (short pause) You are standing at the top. (short pause) Above you there are only light and sun.(pause)

— Now imagine leaving your physical body behind and traveling upwards into the air. You may like to imagine yourself rising as a cloud, a ray of light, or as pure energy. You merge and blend with the light that fills the sky. (short pause) Be aware of the quality of your light or energy, of how it feels to be one with the light of the sky. (long pause)

— You are experiencing the quality of your own pure energy, the quality of your essence. (long pause)

— Ask yourself now, what is the aim or purpose of this essence in your life? (pause) How can it best express itself? (pause) What does it have to give? (pause)

— Now look down on your life and imagine how it would be if you fully expressed or realized this energy of yours, your essence, in your daily life. (short pause) Picture how your life would be if the quality of your energy was there in everything you did. (short pause) You may need to imagine changes in your lifestyle, your work, your relationships. (long pause)

— You are still merged with the light, but gradually you start to come back down to the top of the mountain. (short pause) There you find your physical body again. (short pause) When you feel ready, enter it— go back into your body. (pause)

— You start walking back down the mountain. (short pause) Be aware of being back in your body. (short pause) Be aware of your surroundings. (short pause) Be aware of what the light is like. (pause)

— On your way down, you find a stone that is special to you. (short pause) You pick it up to keep as a reminder of what you have learned of your essence. (pause)

— As you proceed, be aware of any changes you may want to make when you return, ways you can change your life so that the essence you contacted can shine through. (pause)

— You get to the foot of the mountain and walk back along the path or road to the place where you began your journey. (pause)

— You are back. (pause)

When you are ready, open your eyes and come back into the room.

Guidelines for How to Interpret Your Journey

The "you" in your journey may describe something of your inner hero. The terrain you encountered may describe something of your current state of mind, your immediate circumstances. The mountain is taking you away from this, up onto a higher plane, both literally and symbolically. The height and ease or difficulty of the ascent is relevant. People with Sun Saturn or Sun Pluto contacts often image an impossibly high mountain or sheer cliff face, showing something of the inner experience of having such an aspect.

The light we image is central to this journey and represents our essence, our creative force. Contacting this essence always seems to leave participants feeling well, energized, and centered in themselves. When imagining our light, we are more in touch with our essential self, and at such time, any questions we put to ourselves will either elicit crystal clear answers or seem irrelevant. There is a certainty, a knowing, when we are in touch with ourselves in this way. If we have a pressing question or issue in our life, we can introduce it at this stage of the journey. At any moment, even days or weeks later, we can take some time out to sit or lie somewhere quiet and reconnect back to our image of our light. If we have a particular question, we can pose it and get an answer.

Participants always descend the mountain with far more ease and panache than they climb it. Life is suddenly much easier, and we see it from a new perspective. We have literally risen above the mundane and gained a higher vantage on what really matters to us. Once we have contacted "our light," we can return to this image, our essence, at any time, to recenter ourselves.

The stone we find on the way down is a more tangible representation of our light, our essence, and it strengthens our connection. This is a way of grounding the experience. The stone we imagine may be one we already possess, or it may be an imaginary one. If you already have your stone, or if you find a stone similar to the one in your imagery, it can serve as a permanent talisman for you to draw on. Touching the stone can help you connect back to your light and the feelings of clarity and perspective you felt when in touch with your light.

It is important after visualizing an out-of-body experience to make sure we are back in our bodies. Hence the insistence at the conclusion on feeling ourselves back in our bodies and in touch with our surroundings, as well as being aware of the light, which is now separate and outside of us, as we come back down the mountain. It is always important with guided imagery work to return to the place we start from.

Other People's Journeys

Let us go on to look at the charts and experiences of a man and a woman whom I lead on this journey. Jill was a member of a small group who went on the journey on January 9, 1993. Rory went on the journey on April 16, 1996. Their accounts are reproduced here verbatim, as they were recorded at the time. We can see much more in retrospect when we are distanced from the emotional experience of the guided imagery journey; my comments and interpretation benefit from this. I hope that non-astrologers can bear with the astrological signifiers I have inserted in parentheses in the text. These can be completely ignored by those not fluent in astrology. They simply communicate to astrologers the connections I have made between the participants' journeys and their natal charts. This subject is explained in greater detail in the commentary that follows, which non-astrologers should not have a problem following.

JILL'S SUN JOURNEY

"I'm going on a quest. I start along a road, not tarmac, but hard-packed, in a village—like a French village—sun overhead, warm stone houses, high walls on either side of the road. There are pavements, but I walk along the road, quite fast, a steady tread. (Sagittarius rising, Jupiter in Virgo in the ninth)

"Downhill a little, out of the village, fields on either side, cows in the fields. I see a mountain in the distance and go towards it. I begin to climb. A very steep path, quite stony. (Mars, Sun ruler, trine Saturn) I have to cling with my hands for part of the way. I reach one peak only to find I have to continue along a narrow, flattish path to the real summit. It is very high. (Sun inconjunct Jupiter, Neptune conjunct the MC) I feel out of breath and very dizzy when I look down, I can feel my heart palpitating. Dark grassy slopes with sheep in the distance—they seem a long way down. It is very windy and clouds are gathering. I have to lie down for a while as I don't like it at all. (Sun in the fourth)

"There is very little space on the peak—it has a narrow pointed top with a small, stony, flat bit where I am. Then the clouds go away and the sun reappears. I climb upwards, out of my body, in a shaft of light, but with wings. I feel very light. I notice lots of other shafts of light shining downwards from the sun to the earth. (Jupiter and Neptune in the 9th, Neptune conjunct the MC) My essence feels warm, light, laughing. (Sun in Aries) Its true expression seems to be to illuminate dark corners. (Sun in the fourth) I have a magic wand that can make things better and happier. (Sun conjunct Mercury, Mercury semi-square Uranus) At first, I think this is something I have to do for other people. (Moon Pisces trine Saturn in Cancer in the 7th) Then I realize I have to lighten the heaviness in my own life. (Sun in Aries)

"When I come down again, back into my own body, I am no longer dizzy and afraid of the height. I can look down the sides of the mountain quite easily without fear. There is a lighter tread to my walk as I come down the mountain, a new determination to go for what I want. (Sun in Aries) I find a stone. It is hand-sized, smooth and oval, but crystalline, golden, streaked brown, and it sparkles as it catches the sunlight. I skip down the path, even though I had to hang on going up—the steepness is no longer a problem. The way back to the village seems quite short and the village houses are bathed in a light that is even more golden than before."

See page 30 for Jill's natal chart. The attention to detail throughout Jill's journeys is a characteristic of her chart ruler being placed in Virgo. Her pace is fast, signified by her Aries Sun, the road well made. We could speculate that her path had been laid down by those before her (the fourth house) and she places herself in a small community, signified by the emphasis in the third and fourth houses.

Jill has difficulties climbing the mountain and suffers vertigo. Climbing the mountain reflects our ability to realize our ambitions and to be in touch with the spiritual realm. Vertigo could symbolize Jill's fear of overreaching herself, a fear of losing touch with the earth and her roots, signified by her fourth house stellium. Her potential to overreach herself, to lose touch with her limitations is signified by Neptune on the MC. The Moon square to Uranus is an aspect that is often found in those with a pervasive sense of anxiety, so this could also contribute to the vertigo. Later, Jill imagines that she has wings, signified by the Sun conjunct Mercury, and from this point on in the journey her fears have vanished.

Throughout this journey Jill juxtaposes the light side of her character with the dark, the paradox of having a midnight Sun in Aries, obscured from view, at the darkest hour in the brightest sign. Jill's chart contains many echoes of this paradox, with Sagittarius rising, yet Jupiter in self-effacing, humble Virgo. The Moon in compassionate, sensitive Pisces, yet conjunct Mars, the planet of self-assertion, indicates that Jill is likely to be emotionally intense and volatile. With her stellium in Aries in the fourth house and Mars, the Sun ruler conjunct the Moon and in Pisces, Jill has a tendency to become waterlogged, to get bogged down by her feelings, losing the quickness and lightness of her stellium in Aries, but in this journey she connects to this positive, life-affirming side of herself.

RORY'S SUN JOURNEY

"I felt like I ought to be a knight, with a white horse. I carried the spirit of a conquering knight—but not the form. The form was me—stout walking shoes and a warm jumper—which made up for no armor or sword, but not the horse." (Moon opposite Jupiter, Sun in Virgo opposite Saturn)

"I was traveling down a clean limestone street. It was a past time, perhaps Roman. All was neat and homogenous. It was a bright day and felt like it was early in the morning because the street was quiet and empty. (Sun in Virgo in the twelfth) It felt like I was on my way out of town. I could see open blue sky in front of me.

"The scenery has changed now. A long, neatly crazy, paved path stretches in front of me. What can only be described as a thicket of non-blooming roses lines each side of the path as far as the eye can see. Closer inspection reveals that the thicket has engulfed the former plant life and general scenery. The tendrils have wrapped themselves around remnants of rusty, white railing uprights that can be made out here and there. (Sun conjunct Pluto in the twelfth) Trees with flaking bark on their dead trunks have been engulfed too. The ground level looks dark and sterile.

"The thicket had a dense, dark, dead feel. (Sun conjunct Pluto in the twelfth) It was a relief to reach the mountain, large and green. My vista was wide, taking in surrounding hills and valleys, pinpointing houses. Something here felt strange, too, though. The conical shape of the mountain. The unvarying green over its whole surface. Suddenly

I felt like I had walked into the set of Greendale from the clay animation children's series Postman Pat. It all felt false. For a start, the mountain was nigh impossible to climb. Too steep and slippery, it felt like it was made out of tin. (Sun conjunct Uranus) In the end, I decided the only way was to chisel out hand- and foot-holds and gradually edged my way up. (Sun conjunct Uranus opposite Saturn)

"At this point, I decided that I didn't like the mountain I was on and transferred myself to Cader Idris, the second highest mountain in Wales and probably the highest I have ever trekked up. Cader, as it is locally known, is a beautiful mountain with some of the lower slopes retaining relic ancient woodlands, rich in species. It is a fair slog to the nearly 3,000-foot summit and once on the top, the views are breathtaking. Sun on my face, air in my lungs, a cooling wind in my hair and on my face. (Sun in Virgo opposite Saturn)

"Like a ghost I slipped into the blue of the sky, trying to blend for a while and then finally blending into the deep, flawless blue of the clear sky. I felt like I had an invisible shimmer about me. I started to zip around from one position to another like a small bird darting here and there. I relished the aerial view for a moment and then decided to take in other views from my privileged position as part of the sky and light.

"I chuckled at having such a joyous attribute as provider of light to all who fell under me. I felt like the wind. Invisible, clear, and full of life. I saw waterfalls, woodlands, and crags in places that don't exist anymore—the wilderness as it used to be. I felt at one with the world. (Sun in the twelfth)

"The thought of my 'normal life' felt like another world. The thought of asking my light to penetrate the darkest corners of my life felt unthinkable, as if I would not want to expose something so pristine to something so degenerate. (Sun conjunct Pluto in Virgo) Initially I felt like there was none of my light present in my day-to-day life. Looking deeper than surface level, it could be found in almost all areas of my life. The dark feelings surrounding the day-to-day monotonous aspects of my life were not as all-pervading as I had thought at first. I was reluctant to come back into my tired, broken, and sullied body. (Sun Pluto Uranus conjunction opposite Saturn)

"Walking down Cader was lovely—a feeling of elation at the ease of the return descent, marveling at how easily the ground that I cover made me break a sweat earlier. By a gate, I pick up a sharp axe-head-shaped stone, broken in a magical way so as to create a fine cutting edge, and a slightly thicker upper, to enable to grip. The cutting edge was flinty and colored, a natural color variation, a bit like the color of oil on water, but not as strong. (Sun in Virgo in the twelfth) I looked briefly for another stone, perhaps round and gold, something more pretty than an axe perhaps. (Libra rising, Venus in Libra in the first) I looked back at my axe head and it was now V-shaped. Supposedly more interesting. I had lost the uniqueness of the axe head in looking for something aesthetic, but ultimately unusable.

"I returned along the same path I had come, avoiding Greendale. I returned to the start of the thicket, but not the town. I see my light chinking through here and there in many areas of my life. I think the capitalist system stinks, and I don't like the way the resulting society has evolved. Asking my light to overthrow capitalism and change society seems to be asking a lot. Who knows what can happen, though." (Sun Pluto Uranus conjunction)

See page 35 for Rory's chart. Rory starts his journey imagining himself as a knight, but without the lance and horse he expects to have. His high expectations, signified in his chart by Sun conjunct Uranus and Moon opposite Jupiter, are disappointed, shown by Sun opposite Saturn. His reality does not fulfill his hopes. The lack of a lance and horse also describe his feelings of impotence and disempowerment, shown astrologically by the Sun conjunct Pluto. This conjunction symbolizes his propensity to grapple with power issues, to reach a feeling of powerfulness through struggling with feelings of powerlessness.

The railings can be seen to represent the boundaries in Rory's life, the Saturnian limitations within which he has to live. The theme of death and engulfment provides a glimpse of some of the difficulties Rory experiences, signified by the Sun in the twelfth conjunct Pluto. His imagery of the rose thicket is reminiscent of the sleeping beauty fairy tale, which can be seen as representing the transforming process of life itself, another way a Sun Pluto conjunction can be experienced.

Rory states earlier that when he is on his way out of town, he has a sense of a purpose and destiny. However, his mountain, which connects with his ambition, "all felt false," a manifestation of the unrelatedness of Sun Uranus. He can't climb the mountain, which reflects the fact that he is unable to realize some of his ambitions in life—they lack reality. He makes a determined and serious attempt before admitting defeat and switching to something attainable.

This part of Rory's journey reflects the sheer impossibility of life, the extent of his struggle and difficulty, and how hard he works to get on. We would not expect life to be easy for someone with a Sun Uranus Pluto conjunction opposite Saturn, and we see him grappling valiantly against his own grandiose expectations, signified by Uranus, and the unbearable "dense, dark, dead," and "sterile" feelings that he has when he gets in touch with reality, signified by Pluto and Saturn.

When faced with the impossibility of life, Rory manages by remembering things he has conquered before—a real mountain he has actually climbed rather than an impossible hypothetical one—and when his ambitions are fulfilled, he achieves clarity and perspective—his view from the top of the mountain is vast. In this imagery we see the positive manifestation of his Sun opposite Saturn: sticking to things he knows he can manage, relying on his past achievements, and a positive Sun Uranus then comes into play by granting him perspective and clarity.

At times, Rory touches on a transcendental experience, another manifestation of the Sun in the twelfth house conjunct Uranus. Everything is so
idyllic, there is a garden-of-Eden feel. This can be seen as partially compensatory for how hard life seems to him, and this idealism contributes to his
difficulties. He has such high hopes and dreams, anything short of them
leaves him dissatisfied. We can see the interplay of various chart factors at
work here: the Moon in Sagittarius opposite Jupiter expects so much, is so
expansive and ebullient, but his Sun opposite Saturn keeps him pinned to
reality, the wheel of life, and suffering. The Sun Uranus conjunction contributes to the idealism, the inspiration and genius, but again Saturn and
Pluto weigh him down, and he must deal with the real world and all that it
brings. Rory seems to have a memory of a time before, when everything was
idyllic—possibly memories of the womb—before the inner turmoil began
that the Sun Uranus Pluto conjunction signifies.

Rory speaks of being a "provider of light," which reflects his need to be
of service, something likely to be particularly important to him with the
sixth/ twelfth house axis as well as the Virgo/Pisces axis emphasized in his
chart.

The stone Rory first finds is flinty, sharp, and broken in a magical way
with beautiful colors, but he then looks for something prettier. Here is
something not perfect, yet useful, with its own unusual beauty. This
reflects a step towards greater self-acceptance. Yet by hesitating, Rory loses
it and ends up with neither stone, a painful reminder that when he tries to
prettify aspects of himself, he loses touch with what he has that is real and
valuable. This is what happens when he looks for something idealized,
rather than trusting his first impressions, his intuition. We can connect this
to his Libra rising, an aesthetic approach to life, which can undermine his
practical Virgoan side.

Rory ended this journey with concerns far beyond the personal (possibly projecting some very personal, but unmanageable feelings out onto the
world), leaving him in touch with his idealism, as well as feelings of powerlessness. He recognizes on this journey that there is a light side to him as

well as a dark, and the dark contains his despair, hopelessness, and feelings of disempowerment. After Rory had been on this journey, it seemed clear that he would benefit from the Pluto journey, so we arranged for him to go on it. Rory's Pluto journey is included in Chapter 11.

These two accounts begin to show how differently the Sun guided imagery journey can be experienced. Two people with the same Sun sign will also have completely different journeys. It is not just the Sun sign that creates the differences. The house position and aspects to the Sun can at times be more important. In fact, the whole chart gets constellated.

I mentioned earlier that the Sun symbolizes our individual hero. Of the two examples above, Rory's was the clearer. In general, men seem to find it easier to connect to this aspect of themselves. Nevertheless, Rory's knight lacked his lance and horse, so was more of an anti-hero (as befits someone with a Sun Pluto conjunction) showing Rory's feelings of disempowerment. Women will often imagine themselves as male in the Sun journey. One woman was an armored man, a rather defensive hero figure. Another woman was at times an athlete and at other times a silver woman, a personal image requiring further exploration to interpret. For those of you who have a clear image of a hero figure, please do explore this further yourselves.

What is consistent among those who have been on this journey is a feeling of well-being—they are left more at peace with themselves. They connect to their essence and are given an image. For some, the image represents a higher self, a spiritual center.

If you do this journey while you are under challenging transits to the Sun, their influence will pervade your imagery. You may then want to repeat the journey at some later stage, as you will find changes in your imagery which will describe your changed state.

By way of explanation for those without an astrological framework, if we go on this during a time of profound change, then our images may describe the process we are in. We may want to repeat this journey at a later date, when we have emerged from this time of change and may get a more enduring set of images. When we make inner changes, our images change to reflect what we have become. However, outer change in life circumstances may or may not reflect inner change. To some extent, we can assess our personal growth by the development of our imagery.

CHAPTER 3

The Moon

The Moon symbolizes the feminine principle, the yin principle associated with being instinctive, receptive, cool, damp, introspective, negative, and dark. The Moon is synchronous with the unconscious, and is in polarity with and balances the conscious, yang, masculine principle of the Sun. Together they form a whole; neither is complete without the other.

The Moon represents the inconstant, that which fluctuates and is connected to water, tides, change, and growth. It is receptive and responsive, passive and sympathetic, reflective and feeling. The Moon describes our instinctual responses and habits. It rules our home, the past, our memory, our roots, our inheritance and heritage, where we belong, the unconscious and preconscious. All past experiences are held in the memory by the Moon; it rules the mind and our recollections of the past.

The Moon shows our emotional needs, our experiences of mothering, nurturing, and dependency. The Moon mediates between our inner and outer life; it provides the link. For some this "door" between the inner and outer worlds can be jammed. When jammed open, our inner feelings are revealed compulsively and indiscriminately—there is no containment. When jammed shut, our feelings can be difficult to access—we "shut off," and feelings can on occasion burst through in a torrent, like water through a burst dam. Those with a well-developed lunar principle can accurately reflect others and can act as a container for them, can "hold" them psychologically.

Any early trauma, pre-birth traumas, and the fetus's experience of the mother's state during pregnancy are likely to be shown by the Moon's aspects. A well-placed Moon shows an experience of good, secure mothering which creates a sense of belonging and inner security. When adult, this extends to belonging to society and country, to feeling a part of life and being able to take our place in the world. We will have an innate expectation that our emotional needs are okay and will be met, and as a consequence, create rewarding relationships where our needs are largely met.

Without this early positive experience, we are likely to feel our essential needs are unreasonable and excessive, cannot be met, and that there is something wrong with us for wanting such things. While this may well be so by this stage in our life, the problem goes back a long way and needs to be understood within this earlier context.

In the guided imagery journey on the Moon that follows, we return on a symbolic level to the early, oceanic bliss of the womb, and our subsequent transition from the womb into the world. First, a few words on life in the womb and its relationship to the Moon.

The womb is not dark, as many imagine, but light, with muted tones and shadows. Sounds are also muted and resonate as underwater sounds do. Loud sounds will startle a fetus. The mother's feelings and emotions are experienced by the fetus, especially her unconscious. The fetus will pick up on the mother's unconscious and take it on as her own. Our mother's unconscious becomes a part of us, and this is carried forward, buried deeply within us throughout life, conditioning our responses. This deeply ingrained aspect of ourselves is symbolized by the Moon.

The Moon also represents the time after birth, the preverbal time, when we are most dependent and extremely vulnerable and responsive to the conditions we meet. The Moon in the chart and its aspects show how these early conditions are likely to be experienced. Understanding this, we can see from where our habits, unconscious reactions, and responses in life spring.

This early time in our relationship to our mother and our early feeding is the basis, as we grow, of our ability to relate to our world. Built on this early relationship is our ability to nurture ourselves, to get our needs met, to feel okay about our needs. If there is disturbance between us and our mother, this can later become a disturbance in our ability to relate to others. To quote Robert Hand, "The Moon is the matrix from which all life springs, from which we go out to live and be in the world."

In this guided imagery journey we are looking at lunar issues: How comfortable do we feel? Do we feel we belong? Do we fit in? How able are we to get our needs met and to nurture ourselves?

Of all the journeys, the Moon journey most frequently evokes painful feelings. While not everyone who does this journey connects to painful feelings, and some participants have had very happy experiences, you may wish to wait for a more appropriate time if you don't wish to risk being put in touch with these kind of feelings at the moment. For those who do this journey, if you do feel sad and need to cry, just allow your sadness. I recommend you have someone with you to talk through your journey with afterwards.

Before embarking on this journey, please refer to *Some Guidelines Before Going on a Guided Imagery Journey* in Chapter 1 and go through the *Relaxation Exercise* given there.

Guided Imagery Journey on the Moon's Principle

— I want you to imagine that you are sitting by a lake. (short pause)
— The water is calm and still, with occasional ripples from a soft breeze. (short pause)
— There are willow trees and bulrushes all around you, and they are reflected in the water. (short pause)
— They appear to be growing equally up toward the sky and down into the lake. (pause)
— Occasional ripples on the surface of the lake take the trees away, and then they reappear as clearly as before. (short pause)

— By the bank, rocking on the ebb and flow, is a small, wooden rowing boat with a blanket in the bottom of it. (short pause)

— You climb in and curl up and drift across the lake in your cocoon. (pause)

— Puffs of white cloud float by overhead. (short pause)

— The water, trees, and sky all merge together and with you as you are rocked gently by the water. (long pause)

— You are a part of everything around you, and everything around you is a part of you. (pause)

— You are at one and at peace with your world, held and sustained in gentle undulating motion. (long pause)

— With this feeling of being held and rocked in gentle motion, you slowly drift across the water and come to a small river. (short pause)

— You start to float down the river. (short pause)

— You are on a journey. (pause)

— Notice what the weather is like now. (pause)

— You float on to another imagined landscape of your own. (pause)

— Imagine the surroundings, the location, all the circumstances. (long pause)

— Do you feel comfortable here? (pause)

— There are others here. (pause)

— How do they receive you? (pause)

— See if there is someone who is especially here for you. This is an imaginary person, not someone you already know. (pause)

— What are they like? (pause)

— You are to wait here. (pause)

— How does it feel to wait? (pause)

— You are learning to fit in, to become a part of this place. (short pause)

— How does this feel? (pause)

— The things and people around you keep changing. (pause)

— How is this for you? (short pause)

— The person who is especially here for you has a home that they take you to. (pause)

— What is the home like? (pause)

— You enter through a doorway. (short pause)

— You can explore inside. (pause)

— What is it like inside? (pause)

— This is to be your home. (short pause)

— Do you feel you belong here? (pause)

— You are given a meal. (short pause)

— Imagine what it is like. (pause)

— Does it taste good? (short pause)

— Is it enough? (short pause) Or too much? (short pause)

— Do you feel you are going to be alright here? (short pause)

— Find a place that is comfortable here to rest. (pause)

— When you are rested, begin your journey back. (short pause)

— Say good-bye to the person who is especially here for you, (short pause) and go back the way you came. (pause)

— Find your boat and climb back in, (short pause) go back along the river, (short pause) and across the lake (short pause) to the bank. (short pause)

— You are back sitting on the bank. (short pause)

When you are ready, open your eyes and come back into the room.

Some Guidelines for How to Interpret Your Journey

In this journey, the time in the cocoon of the boat, drifting on the lake, merged with all the surroundings, is evocative of a positive experience in the womb, and most participants have a blissful time at this stage. Very occasionally, a participant has felt alarmed by drifting, feeling out of control, and some have imagined or wanted to have oars. In such instances it is always illuminating to note whether we have imagined the oars (or whatever) or not. There is a choice here between following the guide, feeling helpless and out of control, and going against the guide, taking charge, and being in control. When this choice arises for someone on a guided imagery journey, it will almost certainly have relevance for them beyond this and within their life.

The scenario in the first part of the guided imagery is intended to give participants a relaxed, pleasant time. Those who do not experience feelings of well-being are the exceptions. In such instances the basis of such a profound lack of trust will be revealed by the whole chart. Even those of us who have had times of difficulty in the womb will usually have some positive experiences to draw on.

The next part of the journey is a new phase, flowing out of the lake down a river, beginning to create a landscape of your own. The Moon's sign and aspects will often begin to show here. For instance, those with the Moon in water signs or houses tend to create a lot of foliage and undergrowth. Participants with Moon Pluto aspects are prone to imagining a sense of threat, often with eddies, whirlpools, or strong currents. Those with Moon Pluto aspects are also the most susceptible to falling asleep, a way of blocking the process, perhaps because it is too threatening. Those with Moon Saturn aspects may imagine a bleak, sparse landscape, sometimes literally cold with snow, sometimes unpopulated. Those with Moon Uranus aspects will usually rebel against my script and go their own way at some stage on the journey—in fact someone with a strong Uranus could do this on any of the journeys. Those with Moon Neptune aspects generally have a rich and developed imagination, and are among those who produce the most vivid and elaborate journeys.

The river can be likened to the birth canal, and it evokes being born. Rocky formations, high cliffs, narrow entrances may all relate to memories stored from the actual experience of birth. In particular, narrow rocky passages may recall our passage from the womb through the cervical opening into the birth canal, which can be experienced as extremely constricting. If our birth was traumatic and we have not managed to resolve this psychologically, then the trauma will lie dormant within us and affect our attitude toward times of transition and change.

The imagined climate and landscape illuminates the inner climate and landscape. The Moon's sign, house, and aspects, as well as the individual's current state of mind will be revealed. A snowy landscape may indicate a cold room, or there may be a lack of emotional contact or warmth in the person's life. A barren landscape may reveal itself because of current and immediate feelings of isolation and loneliness, or because of the individual's inner, long-term way of being in the world. Such a person may feel undisturbed by this image, as it is natural and normal for them, but it offers them the opportunity to question their inner landscape.

We might also create this kind of image if our life is too crowded or overwhelming; a barren landscape is then something we long to escape to. It could be argued that the busyness of our lives is a defense against inner loneliness.

Coming ashore, and finding people, describes our expectations of how we will be received. This may reflect our arrival into the world—how our parents received us, and what state of mind they were in. We are accessing an expectation that lies below the level of our conscious minds which will color how we "arrive" in any situation.

The person who is especially there for you is intended to evoke a maternal figure, the person we meet first when born. Some participants image a positive figure that is especially there for them, others have rather ambivalent figures, some have downright malevolent ones, and some have no one. These images may echo our early inner experience or may be compensatory.

The gender of the figure is left up to the participant. For some the figure is of the opposite gender, and for some there is a romantic attachment which perhaps indicates the search for maternal nurturing in their romantic relationships.

The next stage of the journey relates to the function of the Moon in adapting, fitting in, waiting, changing. These are all lunar principles. Having created a fantasy landscape involving others, it is important to see how well we are able to function in this situation. If we have created a situation that is uncomfortable and uncongenial to us, it begs the question, why? There will usually be difficult aspects to the Moon. We may be uncomfortable with ourselves or with our needs, feelings which have their roots in our earliest years. Our fantasy is indicating to us, rather starkly, that we continue to perpetuate this early experience through our unconscious expectations of how things will be for us. This part of the journey illuminates what difficulties we may have in creating situations that suit us, and whether we need to understand our own needs better.

The next part of the journey, going to the house, is in some ways a repetition. It shows us our ability to find safety and security. Many participants are really surprised by the kind of home they imagine. Some image very grand homes, even grandiose ones. Clearly, this can be explored further. Others have simple homes or idyllic homes. Most participants discover some quality that they would like their real homes to have, even if the specifics don't translate exactly from what they imagined on the journey. Again, anyone who imagines a home they are not comfortable in needs to explore why; this will illuminate some difficulty with the Moon's principle.

The section of the journey involving the meal may reveal, at another level, our ability to receive nurturing. Eating disorders are largely signified by the Moon and can be symptoms of deeper problems around self-acceptance. Anyone who imagines an unsatisfying meal where they are overfed or underfed has inner work to do to discover the roots of these images.

Next, we are searching for somewhere to rest. The images that arise indicate our ability to find safety and security. An ability to create such a space in the imagination indicates a strong likelihood that we will be able to feel safe and secure within ourselves.

Difficulties that emerge on this journey will usually be reflected in the natal chart by challenging aspects to the Moon, IC, or to planets in Cancer. Often, current transits to the Moon, IC, or planets in Cancer will be apparent. Difficulties may be deep-seated problems emerging into conscious awareness for the first time, in which case the contents of the journey can assist us in understanding and unraveling previously buried material.

The difficulties may also be constants, problems we are aware of and take for granted, in which case our images can act as beacons, shedding new light on issues that dog us.

This is not to imply that we discover only difficulties on this journey. For many, there are corresponding feelings of peace and well-being, and a sense of being reconnected to something fundamental within us. Participants are likely to emerge from this journey feeling more grounded in their feeling natures. Even when there have been painful realizations, there can be profound relief.

Other People's Journeys

Let us now look at the charts and journeys of a woman and a man who did this journey with me on February 6, 1993 and on May 10, 1996, respectively. The accounts are reproduced here exactly as they were written by them at the time, with my insertions of astrological significators in parentheses. In the interpretation which follows, I explain more fully the links between the imagery and the charts.

ANN'S MOON JOURNEY

"I am sitting by a lake in a sea-green shift dress of silky material. I have long blonde hair. I am sitting on a white rock by a clear blue, calm lake. The willow trees make the lake greener and softer. I climb over rocks (Pluto rising) to a rowing boat and climb in and curl up under a soft pink blanket. I float out into the lake.

"When asked to merge, I became part of an eye-like hammock, rocking in the base of the eye. Returning to the boat, I travel along a gentle, rippling river, bumping over rocks.

"Gradually, the weather changed and became heavy with dark clouds, and heavy rain pelted down, but very warm. I was soaked, the river narrowed to a gorge, then to a pool surrounded by steep waterfalls, steamy and wet. (Pluto rising, Sun in Scorpio conjunct IC) Strange, little people with large, bulbous heads and stick bodies met me and helped me out of the boat, pushing me up to meet the magician, Merlin, who was waiting for me in his robes, with long, white hair and beard. (Moon in Aquarius in mutual reception with Uranus in

Cancer) He welcomed me as his child and kissed my forehead. He took me to his cave and left me there to wait. I didn't mind waiting since there were lots of interesting things to see, books (old ones), jars full of colored liquids, experiments, strange objects, a font thing for spells. These changed to a fierce dragon which terrified me, and a silver thing which protected me.

"Merlin came back and said he was taking me to his home. The little people ran at my feet as we left the cave and climbed up the mountain to a castle built into the rocks. (Sun in Scorpio on the IC, Moon biquintile Saturn)

"We went under a portcullis. At first it was dark and dank, then it opened up to a massive room, like a cathedral with a long wooden table and benches, stained glass windows, beautiful tapestries on the walls, and a huge, blazing fire. It was all too grand for me. (Leo rising)

"I was hungry and I had a plate of food made up of raw carrots with green leaves on a brown mishmash, like potatoes mashed in gravy. I dipped the carrots in and it was quite tasty, but I couldn't eat it all. (Moon biquintile Saturn) He then asked me what I wanted. I said somewhere smaller and more cozy, to love and be loved. He said I was already loved and should know that. I went to sleep in a monk-like cell and cried myself to sleep. On waking, I went back to the main hall to say good-bye. Merlin was there. He kissed my hands and forehead, and wished me well. He took me back to the boat. The little people were there to see me off. They pushed the boat out and I sailed out of the gloom into the clearer air and bluer skies, back to the lake, climbed out, and sat on the rock.

See page 28 for Ann's chart. Ann has been on all of the planetary journeys with me and frequently transforms her appearance, often imagining herself as a man. In this journey she is creating an archetypal feminine image—she does not in fact have long, blonde hair. This ability to transform her appearance is signified by Pluto rising.

Ann imagines difficulties in the form of rocks early in her journey, another manifestation of Pluto rising. The river narrowing into a gorge, the waterfalls and pool are all suggestive of birth, and while Ann's imagery is not suggestive of trauma as such, Pluto rising does suggest birth may have been traumatic. Ann's imagery is also evocative of her midnight Sun in a water sign, which has a resonance with the Moon as the natural ruler of the IC.

The little people were clearly alien, Uranian creatures, and as such not of the human world. They also have a childlike quality, and we could speculate they are representations of Ann's "inner child," rather underdeveloped and impoverished. Merlin is another Uranian figure who does not respond to Ann's emotional needs, hence his inability to understand properly her question, and his too-rational answer that leaves her alone with her grief. Merlin is waiting for Ann, and can be seen as a rather remote father figure. There is no mother figure in the imagery, nothing maternal except the birth imagery. We can speculate that after birth, daddy was waiting.

Merlin's books and spells can be seen as indicative of Ann's potential to idealize and intellectualize things while emotionally distancing herself. Her Aquarian Moon is more at home in the realm of ideas, and we have in Ann's imagery much to satisfy her interest. What is lacking is on the emotional level, everything is rather cold, and later in the imagery, when Ann goes to sleep in a monk-like cell and cries herself to sleep, she is painfully in touch with her loneliness and feelings of deprivation. Ann is cut off from her own inner depths (Sun in Scorpio on the IC), preferring the world of the intellect (Moon in Aquarius). On this journey she is painfully in touch with the consequences of this. The feelings of abandonment Ann connects to have been established by the early pattern of her relationship with her parents, but are perpetuated now by her own disregard for her inner world.

The food Ann is given indicates her feelings of deprivation. "Raw carrots with green leaves" lack comfort. "Brown mishmash" is like baby food, unappetizing, with no center to it, no heart. Despite this, she finds it tasty, perhaps reflecting low expectations of being nurtured, as well as difficulties in being able to nurture herself.

Ann's dilemma of having emotional depths (Sun in Scorpio on the IC) that she is at times alienated from, is demonstrated in this journey. With her Aquarian Moon, she has escaped the painful feelings of abandonment to become too rational and at times cut off from what her essential nature needs to feel safe and secure. This supposition was later confirmed when Ann went on the Neptune journey (see Chapter 10), which constellated very powerfully her abandoned inner child.

LANCE'S MOON JOURNEY

"The boat drifts. The sun's high and there is no longer any sign of clouds. The sky is powder-blue, and I feel cocooned by the sun's warmth.

"The river meanders until we reach an ancient jungle. Unlike the softness of the willows, these trees by the river bank are massive and gnarled. Their roots penetrate the river bank and extend into the water. Thick vines crisscross among them and hang down until they almost touch the water's surface. (Moon conjunct Saturn in Pisces) There are many birds here. The trees are full of their song. I see small creatures drinking from the river, then disappearing into the jungle's darkness. I know larger creatures are in there, but I am not afraid. I feel anxious. It feels like returning home after a long journey, but I am comfortable. (Sun conjunct Mars in Taurus on the IC)

"The boat floats into a triangle of roots, and on the bank people wait to greet me. They are laughing, smiling, calling my name. There is a feeling of excitement. I love these people, and they love me. (Sun sextile Moon)

"I look among them for a special friend. I begin to feel worried that there is no one special there for me (Moon conjunct Saturn), but then I see her, a jet-black dog with glittering eyes. (Mars on the IC in Taurus) She's my closest friend here. She seems to be ignoring me, but it is an old game we play, and the fact that she's playing it now shows our friendship hasn't diminished. (Moon conjunct Saturn)

"She's trembling trying to hold her excitement back (Moon opposite Uranus), and when she can no longer resist, she barks and runs to my side. We've always been inseparable. (Moon in Pisces)

"I've been told to wait. I feel impatient. There are so many people to see, stories to tell and hear. I want to be connecting to my people. (Sun on the IC)

"I feel natural here. Fitting in is as simple as switching on a light. I know the ways of these people. They're my ways too. (Sun on the IC in Taurus) But I want to tell them what I've seen out in the world, how others live and survive and die. (Neptune conjunct the MC)

"I am meeting people, visiting homes. I'm beginning to feel tired. My dog/friend is at my side always. That never changes.

"Eventually, dog takes me to a home. It is made from wood entirely. It has two floors. The wood's been treated with something and glows with life. This house could have roots like a tree. (Sun in Taurus on the IC) Inside, the furnishings are sparse: wooden chairs around a wooden table, all beautifully carved. The floor is smooth, and a spiral staircase leads to the bedroom upstairs.

"There is a small kitchen area with stove, basin, and cupboards. There is food cooking on the stove; the aroma fills the house. It's mouth watering. (Sun in Taurus)

"I want to personalize the place, make it mine. Pictures and works of art, books, and other bits and pieces need to be added for me to totally belong here. (Sun in Taurus on the IC opposite Neptune)

"The food on the stove is for me. It's chicken soup (West Indian style), with dumplings, yam, cassava, and potatoes in it. It tastes exquisite. I eat too much. I'm bloated, but very content. I feel secure here. I'm going to be fine. (Sun in Taurus)

"However, the one thing I would like is an after dinner spliff. I ask dogfriend if there is any. She pads over to a cupboard and barks softly in front of a particular drawer. I walk to the drawer, open it, and look inside. The drawer's full of weed. The smell is intense. I take enough for a spliff and close the drawer. (Sun opposite Neptune, Moon in Pisces)

"After smoking the joint, dogfriend leads me up the spiral stairs to the bedroom. The bed is a four-poster surrounded by mosquito netting. My eyes feel tired just looking at it. It has been prepared for me. The pillows are fluffed and the sheets turned down. I nestle in the middle and feel supported, yet cradled, by the mattress. Soon, I drift into a deep sleep. (Neptune on the MC)

"I wake up thoroughly rested. Now I have to go. Dogfriend and I say good-bye on the river bank. She sits there as I float away on my journey back to the lake."

See Lance's chart on page 32. Lance journeys to an ancient jungle, which seems to be about the primitive, elemental nature of the unconscious, which the Moon symbolizes. His descriptions of the jungle vividly reflect the rich inner world of a man with the Moon in Pisces and the Sun on the IC. He says "larger creatures are in there," meaning hidden in the jungle, but perhaps he is also referring to what lays hidden within the unconscious. With Mars on the IC, these creatures in the jungle could represent his instinctual side and his aggression. He admits that he feels anxious, but in the previous sentence he says he is not afraid, a contradiction which seems to indicate a denial of fear of what may lay hidden. In the first section we have Lance's delight in his surroundings—the at-homeness of a person with the Sun and Mars in Taurus on the IC—with their primitive nature, as well as some masking of whatever fears Lance may have regarding internal processes.

He arrives to a glorious welcome—he is happy, recognized, and loved. The inner security this imagery reflects is shown by the Sun Moon sextile in his chart. Yet, soon after Lance is doubting if anyone is there especially for him, which reflects the insecurity of Moon Saturn in his chart, and the deep feelings of rejection he is likely to have felt in his early relationship to his mother. A dog is especially there for him, a reflection of his primitive, instinctive, animal nature, signified by Mars on the IC. This is what he can trust in and rely upon within himself.

Neptune on the MC also describes something of his experience with his mother, his longings for unconditional love, his potential to idealize, while Moon conjunct Saturn in Pisces, the sign Neptune rules, echos this longing, yet speak of his vulnerability and disappointment, the impossibility for any mortal to satisfy his needs. There is no maternal figure here. Instead, a dog takes her place. Dogs are totally uncritical, and renowned for giving unconditional love and acceptance, something Lance yearns for. Lance later says of the dog, "We've always been inseparable." He has found someone who is totally there for him, which has to describe his deep longing for oneness with another.

The game dog and Lance play is also interesting, reflecting that on the surface, emotional relationships are not acknowledged. There is a coolness and apparent rejection (Moon Saturn), yet dog is trembling with excitement. This speaks of an inner sense of security, signified by the Sun in Taurus on the IC, which lies beneath the surface. Beneath the apparent rejection, signified by Moon Saturn, is the certainty of a continuing bond.

Lance says, "I want to be connecting to my people," which betrays a sense of alienation and a deep desire to belong and to be understood. The strong desire to connect to his ancestral roots is signified by the Sun and Mars on the IC. He wants to tell them what he has seen out in the world; he needs to integrate his experiences into his deeper sense of identity.

Dog's home contains some delightful, sensual imagery: the simple, natural wood glowing with life, the house with roots like a tree, the simple kitchen, and the aroma that fills the house. All this exemplifies Lance's Taurean Sun on the IC. Neptune opposite the Sun manifests, too, in his need for pictures, works of art, and books. Lance has an artistic, creative side that needs cultural accoutrements.

The bedroom is comfortable, the bed prepared for him, reflecting perhaps the extent to which he has been looked after, as well as his longing for things to be ideal. The spiral staircase to the bedroom suggests that there is not a straightforward route to the place of intimacy and implies that Lance may have difficulties around intimacy.

The fact that the meal is West Indian (Lance's roots are in the West Indies), reflects his Sun on the IC. Lance satiates himself. This fullness, along with the effects of an after-dinner spliff, is reminiscent of the stoned, groggy state of a baby after breastfeeding. Lance, it seems, is trying to recreate this, and longs to return to a state of unconsciousness and feelings of at-oneness he once had. Once, perhaps, everything was wonderful, but things went wrong for him later—there was some emotional deprivation and he now attempts to get back to his original state with his mother. Astrologically, we can see this signified by Neptune conjunct the MC as well as his Moon conjunct Saturn in Pisces.

Lance's imagery is rich and vibrant, reflecting the sensitive and imaginative world of someone with a mystic rectangle involving the Sun, Moon, Mars, Saturn, Uranus, Neptune, and Pluto. This is a quite extraordinary aspect pattern showing exceptional artistic and creative potential, which I have failed to do justice to in my commentary. For the sake of those who are new to astrology, I have focused on the core signifiers coming through in Lance's imagery, but those of you with an astrological background can, I'm sure, see the whole of this mystic rectangle operating.

The first time I led this journey for a group, I was a little anxious as to how they had all got on. The first woman to speak said she had hated it, had not followed my instructions at all, and had in her imagination simply gone home. Understandably, I felt thrown. Perhaps this was not going to work after all. I managed to ask about the Moon's placement in her chart. And then it all made sense—she had the Moon in Cancer conjunct Uranus. Here was Uranus the rebel, defiant as always, coupled with the Moon in Cancer. This participant had gone home: perfect astrological symbolism. Now seemingly untoward experiences on these journeys don't phase me. I just look to the person's chart to make sense of whatever happens.

What the two charts we have looked at have in common is the Sun on the IC, and what the two journeys demonstrate is the extent that the IC manifests in the Moon guided imagery. The Moon has an affinity with the IC, a point in the chart that signifies our inner, private world, our home, our roots, and our past. So in these two examples, the Sun's symbolism has manifested simply because it is on the IC and was being evoked. When doing the Moon guided imagery journey, any planets found on the IC, in the fourth house, and in Cancer are likely to be evoked.

What differentiates our two examples is the Moon's phase. Ann is a first quarter type and Lance a last quarter type. Both phases are characterized by crisis, but there is a difference in orientation and motivation in the world. We can see this in their imagery, in that Lance can take for granted many of the things Ann has to struggle with; her Moon's phase requires action while Lance can expect things to come to him—he has other priorities.

In many ways, too much analysis of these journeys defeats the object. They are a right-brain experience and speak to the feelings and imagination. The participant experiences a "felt" understanding, an emotional "aha." Afterward the many layers of meaning can filter through gradually. A process has begun that can provide a more conscious understanding in time.

CHAPTER 4

Mercury

The planet Mercury governs our capacity to think and understand. Its placement in our chart describes the way in which we take in information and process it, and the level of our ability to do so. It shows the way in which we communicate. Mercury can be complicated and elusive, its meaning difficult to grasp, which is perhaps why its importance is often underestimated, even though the planet's influence pervades and affects all aspects of our life.

Mercurial energy is light and quick. It is fun, playful, witty, mischievous, irresponsible, and amoral. In the tarot, the Fool and the Magician are Mercurial cards. Mercurial energy is inquisitive and curious, childlike and innocent, and it is expressed by the trickster and mimic.

Mercury links and connects—it is the facility to join separate entities. It forms an interconnecting network which brings things together; for example, in the human body, Mercury rules the nervous system along which messages and impulses are passed and received. In society, Mercury rules transport and communication, our road networks, our postal systems, telephone services, radio and television and newspapers. Mercury is like a radio antenna sending out waves that are transmitted far and wide.

Within the individual, Mercury governs the ability to join with others or to sever connections. Mercury can link or separate. What we choose to communicate of ourselves to others defines how connected or disconnected we feel with them. Relationships may break down altogether if people cut off from each other and refuse to speak. Yet, if two people air their differences, they may develop an awareness of their separate identities without destroying the relationship.

Mercury rules our ability to translate our experience into language, which enables us to share our experiences. Language is a system of symbols, and Mercury describes our ability to comprehend and juggle these symbols. A word is not an entity in itself, but rather a symbol whose meaning is shared by people who speak the same language. So *la maison* will have little meaning to you unless you speak French, whereas *the house* has a similar meaning to everyone who understands English. Without this ability to create and understand symbols, culture would not exist. We all have our own subjective experience of any situation, and Mercury governs our capacity to communicate those individual perceptions. (This communication can either bring people together or emphasize their separateness.)

Mercury rules our ability to express ourselves. People with a well-functioning Mercury can put themselves across and be heard and understood by others. They can communicate who they are. In this sense Mercury is the messenger of the Sun, the Sun representing the essence of a person. Mercury's function is to convey our essential ideas and beliefs to others, and to assimilate and integrate others' ideas into our understanding. New ideas thus become a part of us; we take them on as our own.

Mercury describes our ability to discriminate and analyze. We use our Mercury to look at the details of a situation and to assess things accurately. For example, as astrologers interpreting a chart, we must take the chart apart and look at all the components and understand them individually before we can synthesize. We need to understand the parts in order to understand the whole. Our ability to do this, and the way in which we do this, will be governed by Mercury.

The guided imagery that follows presents various symbolic scenarios that put us in touch with Mercury's principle so that we may see how this principle operates within us. Before you begin this journey, please refer to *Some Guidelines Before Going on a Guided Imagery Journey* in Chapter 1 and go through the *Relaxation Exercise* given there.

Guided Imagery Journey on Mercury's Principle

— Imagine you are a small bird. (pause)

— You have total freedom of movement. (short pause)

— You can glide in the air currents, hover, alight where you want, and take off when you wish. (pause)

— You are intensely curious to explore your world, though you tend to stay within a localized area. (short pause)

— Many other birds, as well as other animals and people, share your neighborhood. (pause)

— You live by your wits, alert to dangers and quick to grasp opportunities. (pause)

— Your senses of sight and sound are vital to your well-being and survival. (short pause)

— How good are your senses of sight and sound? (pause)

— Are you quick enough, sharp enough? (short pause)

— Who gets the worm first? (pause)

— It's nest-building time, and you're very busy collecting bits and pieces to weave your nest. (pause)

— Where do you go to get things? (pause)

— Where do you build your nest, and what is it like? (long pause)

— Within the bird Kingdom there is a King and Queen, and their courtiers, who each play a special role on behalf of the King. (pause)

— Your role is to be spokesperson for the King. (pause)

— There is a bird language which consists of far more than spoken sounds. (short pause)

— Your language includes signs and symbols which, all added together, convey meaning. (short pause)

— It is for you to understand and convey your King's messages and instructions to others in the neighborhood and to get their messages back to your King. (long pause)

— At times, it is difficult, as the courtiers and the Queen also have messages they want you to convey, and you have to decide whose get priority. (short pause)

— Whose do you choose? Whose messages come through to you most clearly? (long pause)

— Can you understand your instructions and convey them? (short pause)

— Can you get your messages back? (short pause)

— Are you heard and understood? (short pause)

— Is the King pleased with you? (short pause)

— When you are not delivering messages or building your nest, you like to play. (pause)

— You particularly enjoy making mischief, playing tricks, relying on being quick-witted. (pause)

— What kind of tricks do you like to play? (short pause)

— How bad do you dare be? (pause)

— Do you get caught, or do you get away with things? (short pause)

— You find it hard to rest, as you are always full of ideas of things to do, and you are at your best when active. (short pause)

— What do you like to do the most? (long pause)

— If you are flying or gliding, it's now time to land, and to stop whatever you've been doing. (short pause)

— You are no longer a small bird. You are back as you were. (short pause)

When you are ready, open your eyes and come back into the room.

Some Guidelines for How to Interpret Your Journey

Small birds are light, quick, and nimble. In this journey you are asked to imagine yourself a small bird as a way to connect directly to the lightness, quickness, and agility of the Mercurial principle. This part of the journey generally has an exhilarating and liberating effect, opening you to new possibilities by presenting a different viewpoint and perspective.

You are asked to stay within a localized area and encouraged to notice the activity of this neighborhood. This may well show more of your third house rather than Mercury, although the way you perceive and what you select to pay attention to is likely to be described by your Mercurial placement.

Our five senses are ruled by Mercury. For a bird, sight and hearing are essential to survival. You have an opportunity at this stage of the journey to see how well these two senses work for you. You might realize that they are not working as well as you would like them to. Or you may be delighted by your alertness.

Nest building brings in the lunar principle, but insofar as your dexterity and adaptability are shown, Mercury is signified. In working with these journeys, both the placement of the Moon and Mercury seem to come through. The location of the nest sometimes seems to be described by Mercury's house position, sometimes by the Moon's, although other chart factors may come into play.

Language is clearly ruled by Mercury; being able to communicate and be understood are essential functions of the Mercurial principle. In this journey, the King is intended to represent the Sun in a person's chart, the Queen the Moon, and the courtiers the other planets. However, it is important to interpret this loosely and to explore what the King, Queen, and courtiers mean to you, individually.

Insofar as the King represents the Sun in a person's chart, it is essential to be able to communicate his messages. If the King's messages get drowned out by those of the courtiers and the Queen, it may indicate that you have problems communicating what you really think and believe. If the dominant message you hear is from the Queen, and she is represented by the Moon, then your communication will spring from how you feel. You may be primarily *responding* and *reacting* in your communications. If this is the case, you will be able to communicate sympathetically with others, but will get buffeted about and lose track of what you really think. What you communicate will not accurately convey who you really are, hence you will feel misunderstood. The same will be true if you are predominately communicating the messages of the courtiers. The courtiers represent the various planets, and therefore different principles in the character; they will have important messages to convey, but these may not be the messages of your authentic core.

In this part of the journey you are asked how able you are to pass on messages and convey others' messages back. You may have a problem with, or a lack of interest in this function, which can illuminate problems in communication. You may suddenly realize where you are "going wrong." You may not be able to right this immediately, but at least insight is the beginning to understanding a way forward. You can begin to listen for your "King's" communication and try to quiet some of the clamor of the other voices. You may begin to see why you feel misunderstood, as well as how you misunderstand others.

The final part of the journey takes you into the "trickster" aspect of Mercury. Some people positively revel in this part of the journey, and a delightfully gleeful wickedness comes through. For you, this aspect of Mercury may not be strong, but you nevertheless get the opportunity to get in touch with this playful, irreverent aspect of yourself.

OTHER PEOPLE'S JOURNEYS

Let's look at the accounts of two women who did this journey with me on March 6, 1993. What follows are their verbatim accounts, and I have inserted astrological signifiers in parentheses retrospectively. The analysis following each journey benefits from hindsight and perspective.

ELISE'S MERCURY JOURNEY

"I am a little sparrow, quite plain. There is no color on me whatsoever! Everywhere there are very tall trees; everything is very green, but high above me I can just about see bits of blue sky poking through. (Mercury in Pisces in the ninth)

"I am very attached to the ground, and *there is no chance to fly whatsoever!* This is because I am very frail and my leg is broken, so I am having to keep hopping around to try and get scraps of food. (Mercury in Pisces, No Air)

"I am in the woods, and there is no chance of flying. The worm keeps disappearing, and it seems I have no chance of getting it. I'm much too slow.

Another bird comes along and decides to carry me up to a nest in a nearby tree. I feel I don't belong here and feel very uncomfortable. Suddenly, I fall out of the nest to the ground. (Mercury in Pisces)

"I can see squirrels around me. The other birds seem to fly in great masses, flying above me. I am very much alone. (Mercury in Pisces)

"I find myself in a clearing, out of the forest, with a green hill. It is quite beautiful. I am then eaten by a big cat which sees me and pounces. (Mercury inconjunct Uranus)

"I come to life again—as the journey goes on—and I can see these two large, black eagles. I am loyal to both of them equally. I do not seem to be making much sound, but I am very busy attracting their attention. My efforts seem to be basically physical, i.e., dancing in front of them and pecking at a tree (a bit like a woodpecker). *I am trying very hard to keep my position with these birds.* (Mercury square Jupiter)

"I am drawing attention to the eagles, and then the other birds can come and give them food. I am extremely loyal, and they are attached to me. I can see and hear okay, but physically I am still very frail. (Mercury in Pisces)

"I am suddenly in a pond where there are big lily leaves. I am dancing from leaf to leaf and drinking in the water and playing. (Mercury conjunct Venus)

"However, I fall into the pond and then a frog eats me. I feel a bit happier than before, and quite enjoyed playing in the pond. I was also looking for food, which is very important. However, it really feels okay to be eaten. It's as if everything then can stop—I can stop trying." (Mercury in Pisces square Jupiter)

See page 29 for Elise's chart. Elise was extremely distressed by this journey, in which she is in touch with a vulnerable and less developed part of herself. First of all, she is a very plain sparrow, she has lost all the color of her Leo Ascendant and Aries Sun on the MC, and finds herself quite ordinary. This colorful side of herself is what Elise presents to the world, keeping the more vulnerable part hidden.

There is a lushness to her surroundings which seems to reflect her watery Mercury. She is surrounded by tall trees, and she is literally swamped by her environment, which mirrors how swamped she can be by her feelings. She is in alien territory, the part of her psyche she is unfamiliar and uncomfortable with.

Elise is unable to fly (she has no air in her chart), and she is a victim (a dimension of Pisces), frail and with a broken leg, disabled. Her frailty and vulnerability, along with how small she feels in relation to her surroundings, could relate to her childhood. She is unable to properly take care of herself, and she finds only scraps of food, what others have discarded. She is grappling with an undifferentiated, undeveloped side of herself.

Elise is rescued (another dimension of Pisces) by another bird and taken to a nest in a nearby tree, but, as in so many victim situations, this rescue fails to pay off. She does not feel she belongs here—she does not belong in the airy, intellectual realm either—and she falls out of the tree and finds herself back on the ground.

Elise notices the squirrels, other Mercurial creatures. She feels apart from the other birds, separate and alienated. Her image of them—connected and flying together as a mass—also signified by her Mercury in Pisces in the ninth, only she feels the alienation because she does not identify with this watery aspect of herself. Elise is identified with her fiery side.

Whenever Elise surrenders to some of the more enjoyable sides of Mercury in Pisces, something happens to her. She finds her way out of the forest into a clearing, which she describes as beautiful, where she is eaten by a cat. She is back as the victim. Being eaten can symbolize the plunge into the unconscious, into the undifferentiated, watery realm of her mind.

The eagles, the King and Queen, can be seen as parental figures, powerful and rather overwhelming. Elise badly wants their attention. Her Leo Ascendant and Sun in Aries on the MC come through here in her strong desire to be validated and recognized. She writes in capitals (I've italicized it in the text) that she is trying very hard to keep her position with these birds, implying this is difficult and that she is unable to do so. Elise appeases the eagles, seemingly having to hide her true self. She has become eclipsed by the giant, bright Sun on the MC, her inner parents. The poetic, sensitive Mercury, her inner child, does not get heard. Traditionally, astrologers consider Mercury in the water signs as metaphorically mute. Here, we see Elise's communication is physical.

Elise is concerned about the eagles getting food, though the guided imagery journey does not mention this, asking her rather to convey messages. She is successful in procuring food for the eagles, but has failed to understand what she is actually meant to be doing. Confusion and misunderstanding are classic negative dimensions of Mercury in Pisces, but in Elise's case there may also be a deliberate, quiet rebellion going on, albeit not a happy one. Mercury is sesquiquadrate Uranus, so she would feel free to disregard the instructions to suit herself.

Elise's preoccupation with food is signified by the Moon. Food is a survival issue. To add emphasis to this, her Moon is square to an eighth house Mars. And Elise is twice devoured herself! In this journey she is put in touch with her feeling function, the lunar connections.

In the lily pond, Elise is back reveling in the watery realm—the Mercury Venus conjunction comes through in sheer pleasure and dancing—but once again she is eaten. Her communicative, playful spirit is lost to her. On some level, it seems Elise has a desire to be consumed, as if being eaten is her way of surrendering, of becoming one with an oceanic world.

"I was a bird—first a baby sparrow and then a swallow. I was flying high, high in the sky. I lived by the sea (Neptune conjunct the MC) in a hot country. The beach was very sandy and stretched for miles. Behind me was a city. I think I was in Tel Aviv. (Mercury in Sagittarius)

"I skimmed along the surface of the sea, diving under sometimes to catch a fish. I knew I had to be careful of the gulls, so I made sure I did it when they weren't about. When the other birds were diving for a fish, I went off by myself to another part of the sea to search alone for fish. (Mercury in the twelfth house)

"My nest was in the cliffs by the sea. (Mercury sextile Neptune) It was well hidden—comfortable and dark inside. (Mercury trine Pluto) The entrance was covered with twigs and things, so no one knew it was there, except me. (Mercury in the twelfth house) When I went into my nest, I went through the twigs, like going through a curtain.

"When I was making my nest, I came back to my flat to collect twigs and bits. My cat Froggie was watching me.

"I felt very anxious when I realized I was to be spokesperson for the King. I knew I didn't understand the symbols and language properly, so I asked the King if he would wait a couple of weeks while I studied it, and he agreed. For the next few weeks I locked myself in a room and studied morning, noon, and night. I wore a mortar board and cloak all this time. (Mercury sextile Saturn)

"Eventually, I was happy and ready to start. But everyone was talking at once and I couldn't catch what they were saying. I felt really over-whelmed and kept asking them to speak one at a time, but I appeared to go unheard. (Mercury in the twelfth house)

"Eventually, I flew into the air above them and shouted at them to stop. (Mercury sextile Mars and Saturn) They all stopped at once in midsentence and looked really surprised, and I asked them to speak one at a time.

"The Queen's messages were the easiest and clearest for me to understand, and I translated hers first.

"The King seemed reasonably pleased with me, but said he'd felt quite impatient, as firstly he'd had to wait a few weeks for me to understand the language, and then, when I understood, he'd had to wait until I stopped everyone babbling and interpreted one person's message at a time.

"When I was playing, I was flying round and round teasing my cat and swooping at him. Sometimes I would sit just out of his reach, and we'd watch each other, and then, just as he was about to pounce, I'd fly off and peck his tail. (Mercury sextile Mars, trine Pluto) Also, I played a lot in the bird bath and sunbathed, sometimes with other birds. But after a while I'd get bored and fly off by myself." (Mercury in the twelfth)

See Olivia's chart on page 34. Olivia starts as an ordinary sparrow and quickly upgrades to a swallow, a bird renowned for the way it soars in the sky and migrates, a definite Sagittarian inclination (Olivia has the Sun and Mercury straddling her Ascendant in Sagittarius). She quickly enters into the spirit of this journey and into an airy dimension. The hot, sandy location she finds herself in reflects her fieriness. The emphasis here is on Sagittarius and, especially important, on its ruler, Jupiter, which is also in a fire sign, Aries in the third house, the house with loose associations to Mercury. Being by the sea shore signifies Olivia's twelfth-house Mercury, and angular Neptune.

Olivia senses danger from the gulls, and her fears are justified. The Great Black-backed Gull, a common variety found in the UK, is in fact a callous murderer of other sea birds, not even eating all it kills. The danger is signified by sextiles from Mercury to a Mars Saturn conjunction and a trine to Pluto. Her Mercurial side is under threat of annihilation. In the face of threat, Olivia withdraws into solitude, as is the wont of Mercury in the twelfth. The need for solitude seems to equal the other side of the coin of communication. Olivia communicates and then withdraws.

She soars high in the sky and skims the surface of the sea, representative of the different ways she comprehends things and communicates. "High in the sky" could represent the intellectual realm or a twelfth-house propensity to comprehend the spiritual/mystical realm. "Skimmed along the surface of the sea" could represent a watery or feeling realm in her understanding, backing up the idea that Mercury in the twelfth enhances comprehension of the intangible. Or it could reflect the Sagittarian potential to skim, to be superficial. It could relate to all these levels and meanings simultaneously.

Another dimension of Olivia's twelfth-house Mercury and its trine to Pluto is the hiddenness of her nest, the fact that it was dark inside and that to enter her nest she passed through a "curtain" of twigs. She created a threshold, a place of transition from outer to inner. She returned to a familiar locality to collect twigs, and her pet cat in real life appeared at this point in her imagery. We can speculate that this realism is signified by Olivia's Mercury Saturn contact, and her sixth house, which rules small animals, has Gemini on the cusp, so is ruled by Mercury.

Olivia's anxiety about her role as spokesperson is again signified by Mercury Saturn. She takes her role seriously and prepares thoroughly, but her anxiety to do her job well turns it into extremely hard work. This amount of arduous preparation is what Olivia needs to feel adequate. Once ready, Olivia is still experiencing difficulties; she feels overwhelmed and is unheard, a familiar experience for those with Mercury in the twelfth. She then expresses another dimension of Mercury Saturn and commands some authority.

The King says he felt impatient with Olivia, signified by the Moon Mars conjunction, but given what's gone on, it appears he's actually been extremely patient and tolerant, signified by the Sun square Jupiter. Olivia hears the Queen's messages most clearly and translates hers first. The conflict between the King's and Queen's messages is shown by the Sun Moon square, with Olivia perhaps identifying, as a woman, with the Moon and the

Queen more easily. The King, signified by the Sun in easygoing Sagittarius, is fairly relaxed about it.

The King and Queen are also representations of Olivia's internalized parental figures, rooted in her experience of her actual parents. We could deduce from her imagery that her inner father is a hard task master and that she works hard to please him, to satisfy his demanding standards. This is shown astrologically by the Mars Saturn conjunction—Mars, as ruler of the IC, representing the father—along with the high expectations of Sun square Jupiter. The Sun square Jupiter also shows the father's tolerance. The mother is represented astrologically by the Moon and by Venus, the MC ruler. Venus and Mercury are semisextile, confirming the ease of communication between Olivia and her inner mother.

Olivia's play is full of mischief. She really takes delight in daring exploits and plays dangerous tricks on her cat, signified by her Mercury Mars Pluto contacts. She dices with death. She also returns to her fiery nature, enjoying sunbathing and playing in the birdbath (her twelfth house). It is interesting to see that when she is bored, it is with others, and she flies off to be by herself.

In these two journeys we've seen how Mercury is experienced by the two participants, and how not only Mercury but the other chart factors come alive, and we have a glimpse of the ways the aspects are lived.

I purposely used Elise's account here, although it is not a typical Mercury journey, as an illustration that painful material can surface on any of the journeys. In all the journeys we are dipping down into the unconscious, and we never know which journeys will touch on our painful issues. It may not necessarily be the planetary principles we associate with the unconscious that will unearth this kind of material. A planet's placement in our chart, along with our relationship to it, will be the determining factors, as Elise's journey demonstrates. Elise did all the journeys with me; this one was the most painful.

My analysis of these accounts makes links back to the chart and touches on some of the psychological patterns that are revealed. As astrologers, we are interested to see the different ways the astrological symbols are lived.

I believe the Mercury journey is of great benefit to the participant. Those of you who have experienced the journey know it can be most illuminating, giving you a glimpse of your inner dynamics, of the way you, without thinking or questioning, experience things. Each idiosyncratic aspect of your journey tells you something important about yourself. What we imagine on our journeys applies in all kinds of ways to our lives. The Mercury journey gives us the chance to observe ourselves deeply.

CHAPTER 5

Venus

Venus is the principle of love and attraction, and its placement in our chart describes both our capacity to love and our openness to receiving love from another. Venus signifies how we go about drawing to us the things and people we love, what pleases us, and where our happiness lies. Venus' position shows, by sign, house, and aspect, the kind of contact we need in order to feel loved on an everyday level. Venus' placement also reflects how we express our feelings of love for another. An analysis of Venus in our chart will contribute to an understanding of the patterns in our love relationships.

Venus brings together complementary entities, creating a unity. This unity creates a whole that is stronger than the separate parts. Venus symbolizes the need to merge with another in order to feel whole and complete—to feel more ourself when at one with another.

Venus seeks the common ground with others and focuses on all that is shared. Venus wants harmony, to be liked and loved by others. Venus can consider others and their feelings first, but when working negatively, Venus can overaccommodate others at her own expense. The automatic Venusian response to requests from others is to say yes; we have to use our Sun or Mars to say no. Venus is conciliatory. It soothes and smoothes, is forever pleasant. In the extreme, this can appear false and sickly. Overpoliteness is the Venusian way of distancing others.

In social and business relating, Venus utilizes its considerable tact and charm. It is diplomatic and good at mediation and negotiation. It can help those from opposite points of view find their common ground and link together to their mutual advantage. Venus' principle can describe our material values and the material things we draw to ourselves, including money.

In personal relationships, a lack of understanding between people—how each is different and hence has different needs is often a cause of pain and difficulty. We want to feel at one with someone we love, to feel merged, and an awareness of any differences can be experienced as alienating and rejecting. Behavior that we experience as rejecting may not have been intended to be. What we need in order to feel loved may be very different than what our partner offers us. Venus placement through the signs, houses, and aspects will accurately describe our different needs and ways of expressing love (see *Love and Sexuality: An Exploration of Venus and Mars,* by Babs Kirby and Janey Stubbs, published by Element Books). An understanding of the different ways love is expressed can help us to develop greater tolerance and acceptance of others. It can be difficult to know ourselves, to be aware of our expectations and assumptions, and to be able to communicate them. Most of us wrongly assume that others are more similar to us than they are. One of the things astrology can show us is the great diversity of human experience. It becomes clear to us that love is not merely one thing. This guided imagery journey on Venus gives us a glimpse of some of our expectations and assumptions in relationships.

Venus' principle has to do with beauty in its deepest sense. Truly great artists connect beauty to a truth that gives meaning. The artist captures a truth and conveys it through artistry so that people understand themselves and their world. The intrinsic ability to convey a truth is what defines art as beautiful. The Venus principle is operating in a painting, a piece of music, or a film in the way people relate and connect to its meaning. Venus' principle is at work when, as we look at certain paintings or listen to a piece of music, a feeling of peace and centeredness pervades us. In this guided imagery journey participants are given an opportunity to get in touch with their feelings for beauty and aesthetics. This comes down, on a more everyday level, to our sense of taste and style in such things as clothes and home decoration.

Venus, in its rulership of Taurus, rules our sensuality. In this guided imagery journey we are introduced to a variety of sensual stimuli to get us in touch with the sensual side of ourselves. In the first part we are introduced to the sensuality of nature, and later to the sensuality of food. Some participants positively luxuriate in all this, while others make little of it.

Before you begin this journey, please refer to *Some Guidelines Before Going on a Guided Imagery Journey* in Chapter 1 and follow the *Relaxation Exercise* given there.

Guided Imagery Journey on Venus' Principle

— Imagine you are in a meadow. (pause)

— It's warm and sunny. You can feel a glow of warmth on your skin. (pause)

— You see some wildflowers, you breathe in their fragrance, and you notice how exquisite they are. It is as if you are seeing them for the first time. (pause)

— You lie down in this meadow and watch the butterflies flutter by. (pause)

— You can smell the earth beneath you; the scent of meadow grass wafts by along with other scents of the countryside. (pause)

— There is a background melody from the birds singing and bees humming. (short pause)

— You bask in the ambience, all your senses pleasantly stimulated. (pause)

— After a while you decide to follow a path that crosses the meadow. (short pause)

— You set off, and gradually the terrain changes. (short pause)

— You look around and take in where this path is leading you. (pause)

— As you meander along, you find a chalice. (pause)

— Where do you find it? (short pause)

— What are its surroundings? (short pause)

— What is the chalice like? (short pause)

— What condition is it in? (pause)

— It is yours to keep. (short pause)

— You spend some time discovering what use the chalice is to you, what function it serves. (pause)

— You take the chalice with you as you continue along your path. (short pause)

— Eventually, you see a house in the distance. (pause)

— What is the house like? (short pause)

— Imagine the outside, its condition and its surroundings. (pause)

— You go up to the house and enter it. (short pause)

— What do you notice first on entering? (pause)

— You begin to explore the house. (short pause)

— What is it like inside? (short pause)

— Be aware of how it is furnished and decorated. (pause)

— The house contains many objects. (short pause)

— Imagine what these are. (pause)

— You notice a painting. (short pause)

— What is the painting like? (pause)

— There is a knock on the door. (short pause)

— You open the door, and standing there is someone you feel instantly attracted to. This is an imaginary person, not someone you know. (short pause)

— What is he or she like? (pause)

— You greet each other. (short pause)

— How does he or she respond to you? (pause)

— You enter a large room together and find music already playing and a table laid for a feast. (short pause)

— Imagine what the feast is. (pause)

— What kind of music is playing? (pause)

— You and your visitor can help yourselves to whatever you want. (short pause)

— What do you eat? (pause)

— Throughout this time you are getting to know each other. (short pause)

— What do you discover? (pause)

— What happens between you? (pause)

— Your visitor has to leave, and you bid each other farewell. (short pause)

— It is now time for you to leave the house. (short pause)

— You can choose to keep your chalice in the house, or to take it with you when you leave. (short pause)

— You take the path back to the meadow. (short pause)

— You are back in the meadow. (short pause)

— When you are ready, open your eyes and come back into the room.

Some Guidelines for How to Interpret Your Journey

The first part of the journey is intended to put us in touch with the sensual side of ourselves. All the stimuli are from nature, and a pervasive sense of well-being and delight in the surroundings is usually experienced. In this part of the journey, the scenarios are carefully presented to evoke an idyllic, yet wholesome Venusian experience. Participants are then invited to imagine their own terrain. The pleasant experience we've (hopefully) had so far provides the foundation for the next stage, where there is more scope for our imagination. Hence, we reveal more of ourselves. This first part of the journey evokes archetypal Venus, whereas what follows will be more personal. Our Venus placement may be apparent in the first part of the journey, but it will emerge even more strongly as this journey progresses.

The terrain we imagine may describe something of our current sensual life. If, after all the lushness, we find our path stony or barren, it could indicate we are not meeting or acknowledging our sensual needs. This could range from a physical relationship, where cuddles and caresses are in short supply, to a personal tendency to ignore our physical well-being in general. An overgrown path may also show neglect of ourselves, but it can also show a rich inner life.

Symbolically, the chalice represents Venus, and its condition—what it was like, where it was found, what was surrounding it, what use it was, and whether it was kept or not—will reveal something of how this principle is operating right now. If the chalice is neglected, this may reflect our current circumstances or state of mind with regard to love and relationships. Whether or not the chalice is considered to be of value can symbolize our attitudes about love and relationships, and when no use can be found for the chalice, this can indicate a similar attitude toward love. The attitude may not be conscious, but in uncovering it through the imagery, those who have an unsatisfactory love life can begin to understand why.

Symbolically, the house we imagine represents ourselves. The condition of the house will reflect our health, our physical, spiritual, and psychological well-being. We shouldn't get unduly worried if a part of our house is collapsing or in bad repair, but simply take a quiet note of what this might be saying about our relationship to our bodies and health. A roof covered in moss could mean we simply need a haircut, or it could mean that we are not thinking clearly, or that we have lapsed in a spiritual belief or practice that once sustained us. It is for us to unravel what the message might be, roughly equating parts of the house to various parts of the body.

Entering the house is equivalent to crossing a symbolic threshold. We move away from our external world into our private and internal world. The state of the house's interior may reflect something of how things are for us on an inner level right now. Once inside, we are asked to focus on all that is distinctly Venusian within a home: the decorations, the furnishings, the decorative objects, and a painting. The Venusian side of ourselves is evoked. As we connect to all that we find pleasing and like to surround ourselves with, our aesthetic taste is revealed.

If we imagine something we find displeasing, what does that mean? What is it that induces us to imagine an interior that is uncomfortable and unattractive? The answer will usually be evident in our chart, providing an important realization as to how a particular planetary aspect can work. But this occurrence is relatively rare. More often, we will be surprised by what we have imagined but take delight in it, realizing something about our taste—and the aspects to our Venus— that we may not have realized before.

The next part of the journey will illuminate familiar relationship dynamics. The kind of person we imagine may be described by quite a variety of factors in our chart. Traditionally, the Descendant and its ruler are important, as is the Sun and Mars in a woman's chart and the Moon and Venus in a man's. However, other chart factors can easily come into play, and insofar as this is someone we feel instantly attracted to, Venus is signified. What is interesting is that it is entirely our imagination that creates whatever ensues, whereas often in real life it will seem to be another person's "fault" that certain things happen. How we imagine we will be greeted and responded to is probably how we set things up for ourselves in all kinds of situations. If these preconceptions don't help us get closer to people that we would like to know better, then becoming more aware is the first step to being able to change things for ourselves.

The feast and music are Venusian pleasure-seeking pursuits. The kind of music and food that we most enjoy will be described in part by Venus' placement (the Moon and Neptune could also be evoked). These pleasure-seeking pursuits are traditionally the accompaniment to love; an intimate atmosphere is evoked whereby our romantic fantasies can be given expression. Participants are invited to let their imaginations loose in an intimate atmosphere with someone they are attracted to. Whatever ensues will illustrate a dynamic which is all too familiar. This part of the journey will reveal some of our expectations and assumptions, and how these create certain scenarios which repeat in our lives. Getting a glimpse of how we create them can be extremely helpful in cases where we are not happy with what we create.

Other People's Journeys

Let us now look at the journeys of a man and women who went on this guided imagery journey with me on April 3, 1993 and May 1, 1996, respectively. The following accounts are as they were written at the time, except for the astrological significators which I have inserted in parentheses. These can be ignored by the nonastrologer and are explained in my commentary which follows.

ELISE'S VENUS JOURNEY

"I am in a meadow with a hill, and it is very green and lush and peaceful, with a stream, and I can see lots of colored butterflies dancing around. There is a white fence and a field beyond with cows, sheep, and a sheepdog. I can smell the aroma of many different flowers— lilacs, daffodils, crocuses, and bright red poppies. (Venus in Aries)

"I find myself on a bike and am riding along a sandy path which takes me to the sand dunes on Maspalomas in Gran Canaria, where I have been on holiday several times. I am right back there, and it feels wonderful and exciting. (Venus in Aries in the 9th, square Jupiter) I am having great fun, and suddenly I am holding a bright silver chalice. It feels a bit like a weapon? (Venus in Aries) At this point in the journey I can't remember what a chalice is, so I'm a bit confused by it, and I throw it out to sea! It falls onto a boat and a sailor throws it back to me! (Venus inconjunct Neptune, Mars in Pisces)

"I go along to the large Maspalomas Lighthouse (Uranus conjunct the Ascendant) with tall winding steps, and when I reach the top, I look out through the chalice at the sea and boats. This is before we are told about a house in the distance. (Venus in the 9th, square Jupiter, inconjunct Neptune)

"My house is a taverna in Maspalomas close to the Lighthouse. The house is very sparse and not particularly colorful—quite boring really. It has a long, winding staircase, and if you stay there, you have to share a bathroom, which I feel is 'roughing it' a bit. There is an old picture on the wall, and when I look, it is of a highwayman on a horse. I wonder what this picture is doing in a Spanish taverna. (Venus in the 9th square Jupiter)

"It is great fun in the taverna downstairs where it is very busy. It sells lovely gateaus, pizzas, and coffees. People are coming and going. I wanted to be downstairs with all the people. (Moon in the 5th in Sagittarius, Venus square Jupiter)

"I meet a special person who is a highwayman, like in the picture. I am very attracted to him and he is dashing and very attractive. I am trying to impress him, especially by dancing around him, although we aren't saying much to one another. I am flirting quite openly with him, and we are eating wonderful paella and seafood. There is lots of Spanish music playing. There doesn't actually seem to be much need of a conversation between us, and anyway it's too noisy, and there's too much going on. (Venus and Mars in mutual reception, Venus in Aries square Jupiter, inconjunct Neptune, Mars in Pisces in the 8th opposite Pluto)

"We are dancing outside the taverna in the street and I am wearing a very bright blue flamenco dress. We are dancing wildly, which is great fun, and really getting on well. (Venus and Mars in mutual reception, Venus in Aries square Jupiter)

"Crowds gather around us to watch. (Sun in Aries on the MC, Leo rising)

"We then get on his white horse and ride off into the sunset! The highwayman takes me to a beautiful hotel which is very grand and white in color. I cannot decide whether this is where he lives or is just staying. I think, 'This is Heaven.' (Venus and Mars in mutual reception, Venus in the 9th square Jupiter in the 5th, Moon in Sagittarius in the 5th)

"I have to leave—very reluctantly. I wonder where I have left the chalice and think it is back in the lighthouse. It annoys me, but I think that's because I don't know what it is! I think it is useless and surplus to requirements, and what is it doing in the journey, anyway? (Mercury sesquiquadrate Uranus)

"I have to go back to the meadow. The highwayman goes off on his horse, and I wonder where he's going. I have a picture of the chalice lying in the middle of a large double bed where I have left it." (Venus and Mars in mutual reception)

See page 29 for Elise's chart. With her Venus in Aries in the ninth house, Elise is very quickly somewhere hot and foreign, a holiday location that she has enjoyed previously. The holiday atmosphere carries through the whole of her journey, as does the feeling of gaiety and adventure. Venus is not only in the ninth house, but square to Jupiter, and resonating with this is the Moon in Sagittarius in the fifth house. Elise's imagery is dominated by these astrological significators.

Although Elise does not remember what a chalice is, and it ends up in the middle of a large double bed, one part of her understands only too well what a chalice symbolizes! Elise describes the chalice as feeling like a weapon, which is an elegant description of Venus in Aries, a sign ruled by Mars, the god of war. Elise's disregard of and disinterest in the chalice does not, in her case, indicate a problem in valuing or being in touch with a feminine side of herself. The mutual reception of her Venus and Mars by rulership and exultation is evident in much of Elise's imagery, from her open flirting to her general level of enjoyment in all her socializing to her riding off with her highwayman on a white horse into the sunset.

Elise's strategy to gain the attention of the man she is attracted to is to be vivacious and dance around him. This is a lovely example of how Venus manifests in such an active and assertive sign. Much of Elise's journey is signified by the emphasis of fire in her chart—she has Leo rising, the MC, Sun and Venus in Aries, and Moon in Sagittarius. It illustrates her unbridled zest for life and enjoyment. She loves being the center of attention and is delightfully open and uninhibited.

The only imagery to cast a shadow was that of Elise's house. It was drab, and it lacked privacy: she had to share a bathroom. Color is clearly very important to Elise, so we must explore what this lack may mean. Her liking of color is linked to her zest for life in general and signified astrologically by the fire emphasis in her chart. This points to an extroverted, vivacious personality, with the color in her life "out there" rather than inside. We can speculate that the lack of color in her home is a lack Elise feels within herself and is running from. So there are some inner feelings of drabness, which, paradoxically, could be signified by Jupiter found in the serious and introverted sign of Capricorn and square to Venus. This would signify the tendency to go to excess to escape feelings of drabness. The lack of privacy in Elise's imagery is something she may actually have difficulty with, given that being alone may pose a threat to her extroverted defense system. Although she does not object to it, her house is actually a taverna, a public place, a fact which further supports this interpretation.

The man in her journey is a highwayman, a character that is typically viewed as a bit of a rogue, yet glamorous. There is much romantic idealism in Elise's imagery—signified by Venus inconjunct Neptune—from her riding off into the sunset to her exclaiming, "This is Heaven." There is also a certain amount of confusion. She doesn't actually know what a chalice is, she doesn't know where she has left it, she doesn't know if the highwayman owns the hotel or is just staying there, and at the end of the journey, she wonders where he is going. Elise is not concerned by this lack of clarity, which is indicative of her trust in life and of her naiveté. While this is charming, it points to problems she might encounter in life if she abandons herself so readily to situations about which she does not have any facts.

The pervasive atmosphere conjured up on this journey is that of someone with a healthy appetite for love and life, and of someone who clearly knows how to enjoy herself. So although there are warnings that Elise may want to heed, she clearly does not have much to worry about when it comes to Venus' principle.

"Peaceful, blissful summer's day in meadow. Aware of all natural activity, smells, and sights surrounding me.

"I get up and decide to follow a path that begins its journey not far from where I am lying. It looks well trodden like a typical country-walk type of path. As I follow it, I can also visualize an overview of myself and my journey. (Sun opposite Uranus) The path is long and winding and meandering down into a more overgrown, woody type area. (Mars in Taurus, Pluto in the seventh house)

"Before I enter the woods, I see something shining in the sun: the chalice. It's lying on its side in a patch of medium-length grass by the side of the path. It is immaculate. Gold and reflective. (Sun opposite Uranus, Moon conjunct Neptune)

"At this moment, another image comes into my mind, another chalice, but it's much older, slightly decaying, silver, uncared for, but very beautiful. Almost more beautiful and appealing than the perfect golden chalice from before. (Sun opposite Uranus, Moon inconjunct Saturn)

"My journey seems to have taken on a duality. I am viewing two different sets of circumstances from the prompts simultaneously. Very like the construction of the film *The French Lieutenant's Woman*, starring Jeremy Irons and Meryl Streep. (Sun opposite Uranus)

"I am aware that the chalice is mine to keep, but I don't feel that it belongs to me. I am uncertain of its practical use. The only thing I can imagine is drinking red wine or milk from the golden one. In both journeys I clutch the chalice tightly and take it with me into the woods. (Venus and Mars in mutual reception)

"Through a clearing in the trees, I first see a lovely idyllic cottage set in the middle of the wood. Thatched roof, chimney smoke, wildflowers growing outside—fairy-tale-like. As I approach it, I'm suddenly transported to my other journey, in which, as I come to the clearing in the trees, I see a huge country house in the distance, like a stately home, a mansion. Still holding the golden chalice, I walk through large iron gates and follow a long, wide gravel track leading to the steps that enter into the house and gardens. A butler stands at the doorway, sullen-faced, waiting to greet me. He looks exactly like Tin Tin's butler, Nestor. (Sun opposite Uranus, Moon conjunct Neptune)

"I walk up the steps and enter the house through the big, white double doors. The butler disappears, and I am left in a huge reception hall with a grand marble staircase leading up to the next floor in front of me. The house is spotless, regal, but completely empty. I have the feeling that I have come to claim it, as if some rich relative has left it to me in their will. (Jupiter in the eighth house)

"Great works of art hang on the walls: the furniture is 18th-century French aristocratic, chaise lounges, etc. As I begin to explore further, I notice one painting in particular. It is huge, dark, and classical, like something by an old master that you would see hanging in the National Gallery—gold frame, etc. (Saturn in Taurus in the second house)

"As I begin to look closer at the picture, it starts to metamorphose and changes into a simple, childlike picture. Suddenly I am back in the cottage of the original journey. The cottage is small and modest, but very warm and comfortable. It is also very familiar and similar to a cottage that I stayed in recently.

"There is a knock at the door. It is a woman. She has just been riding a horse and looks very countrified, very natural. (Moon in Sagittarius) She is very attractive and we flirt, talking to each other as if we know each other, even though we have just met. (Venus in Aries)

"At the same time, I am also visualizing myself answering the door at the great mansion to the same woman. In this scenario she is much more dressy, looking almost princesslike. (Moon conjunct Neptune) We have the same sexual chemistry as in the cottage, although it is a little more reserved. I take her coat, and we enter a huge banqueting hall together. In the middle of the room is a long table stretching from one end to the other. (Stellium in the second)

"Laid out on the table is a great selection of beautiful and rare foods, exotic fruit, etc. At the bottom of the table a string quartet plays Mozart. The atmosphere is dreamlike, filmic, though also very real. We continue our flirtation into an almost erotic eating session, feeding each other suggestively, clothing is removed, etc. But it is not rampant; it is slow and sensual. (Moon sesquiquadrate Venus, Venus and Mars in mutual reception)

"Back at the cottage we sit in a small kitchen/dining room eating a Sunday roast. We sit with all the windows open, letting the summer breeze through the house as we talk. Oasis plays on the boogie box, and as we tuck into our meal, the conversation is quite intense. She is perfect: intelligent, sexy, beautiful, funny, strong, witty, etc. (Moon conjunct Neptune, Venus = Mercury/Jupiter, Jupiter/Uranus)

"In the mansion, we are still bathing in the luxury of the surroundings. We lose control of our senses and end up making love on the table, in the food.

We are aware that there are people in the adjacent room, but are beyond caring. (Venus and Mars in mutual reception, Pluto in the seventh house) Then suddenly she has to leave. I watch as she dresses, we kiss and say good-bye.

"Now I must also leave the house(s). I leave my chalice on the huge banqueting table in the knowledge that someday I shall return to collect it. I follow the path back through the woods and into the meadow, absorbing everything that has taken place."

See Joe's chart on page 31. Joe starts his journey aware that he has an overview of himself, signified by Uranus opposing his Sun. He has perspective on himself and is able to look at himself from a detached standpoint.

The most striking thing about Joe's journey is its duality. He has two stories which run concurrently. This may reflect a duality in Joe with regard to his feminine side, which then affects how he sees women and what he wants from them. In his chart he has a virtually unaspected Venus, which may make it hard for him to square his needs for a relationship and the kind of woman he is attracted to with the rest of his psyche. The only aspect to Venus is a sesquiquadrate to the Moon, which would support the theory that he finds it difficult to reconcile the two images he has of the feminine. Uranus in Libra can also be seen as a signifier of his inability to choose, his ambivalence, and his difficulty in committing to one story line. Libra is ruled by Venus, so we would expect that this might be constellated on this journey.

One story line seems to contain idealized imagery, and the second seems to have more to do with reality. Perhaps Joe is outgrowing his need for idealization, but is not quite ready yet to let go of it. Joe finds his first chalice, the perfect idealized version, before entering the woods, which is to say before he connects to his deeper feelings. The older, uncared-for chalice is the more realistic version, and Joe is able to appreciate it. He realizes it is almost more appealing than the perfect chalice. He is able to see beauty in things which are unstereotypic and not idealized. He takes the chalice with him, reflecting that the feminine principle is important to him. He imagines drinking either milk or red wine from the chalice; femininity is either nurturing (the milk), or stimulating (the red wine).

The film Joe refers to, *The French Lieutenant's Woman*, had two story lines, each involving a relationship played by the same actors, but separated in time by about 100 years. It juxtaposes how society at these different times regards a woman who is not living conventionally and shows a woman who had supposedly fallen from grace in earlier times by becoming involved with the hero. Joe's connection to the film illustrates the duality he experiences on the journey, which has to do with him sorting out his feelings about women.

When in the mansion, Joe is aware of an expectation of an inheritance, which must be signified by Jupiter, the planet associated with expectations, in the eighth house, the house of legacies. It is also interesting that the furniture is French, that is, foreign, as Jupiter rules foreigners. Jupiter is also a signifier—as ruler of the MC—of Joe's mother, so perhaps his legacy is bound up with her and has to do with something unrealized that lies in the mother's unconscious.

Joe's duality is also about art and beauty. He has a different house, different music, different furniture, and a different type of art in the two strands of his imagery. His painting changes from a grand old master into a simple, childlike picture. We could see this signified by Saturn, his chart ruler, in Taurus in the second house, which values tradition, versus his Aries planets, also in the second, which value the simple and naive. One strand of his journey is grand and classical, one comfortable and homely. It seems the grand and classical strand is the idealized version, and by having a cartoon butler, Joe is somewhere aware of the pretense and artificiality of this strand of his fantasy. Joe says "the house is spotless, regal but completely empty," which is perhaps a recognition that his idealization is emotionally empty and meaningless.

Joe imagines the same woman in both strands of his journey, albeit wearing different clothing. Given that everything else changes completely, this seems to illustrate his constancy regarding his love and sexual feelings, and that his dilemma has to do with where to place her and how to value her. There is a similar intensity in both strands, although the idealized strand becomes more sexual, which perhaps indicates that he is more able to express himself sexually where there is more emotional distance.

Joe's dilemma is to choose between the comfortable and homely and the grandiose and ideal. He is struggling to find a way to bring these disparities together in himself. Is it something grand or something reachable? Can happiness be found somewhere very humble and ordinary? This journey seems to be showing him that he can be happy where he is, without the need for grand fantasies.

It's interesting that Joe is uncertain whether the chalice has any practical use. As this has come up on other men's journeys, it may be a common theme for men. I chose to do the Venus journey with Joe because he is a musician, and I perceived him as being strongly attuned to Venus' principle.

He did, in fact, value the chalice and keep it with him throughout the journey. Some men have simply discarded theirs. As the chalice may symbolize the womb, it is not surpassing men may wonder what it is for. Some women experience a similar difficulty on the Mars journey, but often get around this by imagining themselves as men. In my experience to date, men have not changed gender on a guided imagery journey of one of the feminine planetary principles.

What does not come through sufficiently from simply reading these two accounts and my interpretations is how it *feels* to go on this Venus journey. You really must go on the journey for yourself to know what I am talking about. Then the transcripts and my interpretation will really begin to make sense.

CHAPTER 6

Mars

Mars is the principle by which we assert our individuality and express our sexuality. It symbolizes our fight for survival, and our sexuality is strongly connected to the survival of our species on a biological and instinctual level. Mars represents the biological urge for sex—to procreate, to maintain the species. Mars rules lust rather than love, which is Venus' domain. Mars shows in what way we are passionate, how we are aroused, and the specific nature of our sexual desire. Therefore, what excites us and stimulates us sexually will be shown by Mars' placement and aspects in the chart. The kind of lover we want, as well as the kind of lover we are, will be ruled by Mars.

Whereas Venus is the planet of love and attraction and shows how we relate to and accommodate others, Mars shows how we establish our differences and feel separate from others. We maintain our separate identity through resisting the pressures put upon us by others. Our ability to say no and to "hold our own" depends on a well-functioning Mars. Those unable to assert themselves may find that anger and resentment build up and may erupt inappropriately. Our withheld anger leaves us susceptible to depression or may manifest in illness. Anger is then turned inward against ourselves in a self-destructive way. The journey that follows will help all those who overaccommodate others, who "cave in" and find it hard to assert themselves to define personal boundaries. It can also help those with deeper problems such as self-hatred and depression.

The Mars principle is primitive and describes our urge for physical and biological survival and our need to defend ourselves against perceived threats to our being. Nowadays, it is our psychological self that is usually at stake rather than our physical self. Nevertheless, any time we have to take a stand in our life, we can feel as if we are in a fight that our life depends on. We still respond as if our biological survival is in jeopardy.

Mars shows our ability to define our territory and defend what is ours. A male animal marking its territory with its scent is an expression of Mars, combining its sexuality with its territoriality. As humans we tend to defend and define our territory in less obvious ways. For instance, when moving into a new home, many people immediately clean everywhere or redecorate, proclaiming how dirty the new place is. Yet it may actually be cleaner than the place they have just left—but it is not *their* dirt. Cleaning or redecorating is a way of putting their mark on the new place, of making it their own. In a more sophisticated version of the animal marking his territory with his scent, we humans scent with cleaning fluids. We touch everywhere to make the new place our own, cleaning the previous owner out.

Other simple examples of marking territory are leaving a coat on a chair at a meeting or place of entertainment, or spreading a towel on the beach. When we stake a claim to our space this way—in much the same way as our forefathers might have stuck a flag in the ground—we are expressing Mars' principle. How we react if someone has the audacity to encroach on our space will also tell us something about how Mars' principle functions within us.

Mars represents us in action, in the methods we use, the way we do things. Mars rules the muscles of the body and represents the vigor and vitality of movement. A strong Mars will indicate a need and pleasure in physical activity and will be found in the charts of athletes.

Our ability to compete on all levels in life, as well as our ability to win, is signified by Mars. It rules our competitive spirit. Those who have repeated failures in their life may have a psychological block about winning. We speak in a derogatory way of "losers" and may fear this aspect within ourselves, the part that backs off when our goal is in sight. In competitive sports, a winner has to have a ruthless streak in order to have the psychological strength to win. Aside from talent, she has to be able to go out alone, fight for herself, and not be swayed by the feelings of her opponent. In life, this is something that men are perhaps too good at and women not good enough. Mars symbolizes a masculine, yang energy, and men have culturally been given encouragement to embody these qualities and suppress their feminine, feeling, relating side. Women have been encouraged to do just the opposite. This journey is particularly useful to those who want to be more in touch with the assertive, competitive, separate, and individualistic side of themselves. This journey will benefit those needing to make a decision.

Those with a well-functioning Mars enjoy testing themselves through taking risks, through competition, through rising to challenges, and through pushing themselves to improve and extend themselves. Those with a weaker Mars may compete to bolster themselves, because they lack confidence in their own abilities. And those with an afflicted Mars may exhibit bullying tendencies, domineering, or overly aggressive behavior. Those with a strong, well-functioning Mars are confident and do not harbor the insecurities that result in the need to prove themselves.

Before you begin this journey, please refer to *Some Guidelines Before Going on a Guided Imagery Journey* in Chapter 1 and follow the *Relaxation Exercise* given there first.

Guided Imagery Journey on Mars' Principle

— You land safely in a parachute in a place you have never been to before. (short pause) You are alone. (short pause)
— You clamber out of your parachute and take stock of your surroundings. (pause)

— What are they like? (short pause)

— You have with you some items to help you. (pause)

— What are they? (short pause)

— You make a pathway for yourself. (pause)

— What is the terrain like? (short pause)

— The land around you belongs to you, but first you must claim it as yours. (pause)

— How do you do this? (short pause)

— You may have to defend your territory. (pause)

— How do you do this? (pause)

— As you make your way along the path, you find a sword. (short pause)

— Where do you find it? (pause)

— What condition is it in? (pause)

— It is yours to keep. (short pause)

— What can you use it for? (pause)

— What function does it serve you? (pause)

— As you continue on your path, you meet someone you instantly recognize as a rival. (short pause) This is someone imaginary, not a real person in your life. (short pause)

— What is she or he like? (pause)

— What is it about this person that makes her or him a rival? (short pause)

— You feel obliged to make a stand. (pause)

— What do you do? (short pause)

— You and your rival part. (short pause)

— You find somewhere to sit and rest. (short pause) What are you sitting on, and what is your resting place like? (pause)

— As you sit, you start to think about your life. (short pause)

— You have an important decision to make. (short pause)

— What is it? (pause)

— How will you reach your decision? (pause)

— What is your decision? (pause)

— Your rest is over, and you continue to forge your path. (short pause)

— You meet someone you find sexually attractive. (short pause) This is someone imaginary, not a real person in your life. (short pause)

— What is she or he like? (pause)

— What is it that attracts you? (pause)

— How do you react inside to finding someone attractive? (pause)

— How do you communicate your attraction? (pause)

— Does she or he realize, and how does she or he respond? (pause)

— You and this person hear some music coming from somewhere nearby and begin to dance. (short pause)

— What is the music? (short pause)

— How do you dance? (pause)

— What is it like to dance? (short pause)

— A group of people join you. (short pause)

— You have to prove yourself brave to them, and you are given a test of courage. (short pause)

— What is it? (pause)

— Imagine yourself carrying out this test of courage. (pause)

— How do you fare? (short pause)

— Do others see you as brave? (short pause)

— You are to engage in a game of sport. (short pause)

— What do you play? (pause)

— How hard do you try to win the game? (pause)

— Do you win or lose? (short pause)

— How do you feel about winning? (short pause)

— How do you feel about losing? (short pause)

— It is time for you to be on your way back. (short pause)

— You say good-bye to the group of people and the person you were attracted to, and set off back along your path. (short pause)

— You are traveling through territory that is now known to you and belongs to you. (short pause)

— You must decide whether you want to keep your sword or leave it behind. (short pause) If you decide to leave it, notice where you place it. (short pause)

— You get back to where you landed in your parachute. (short pause)

When you are ready, open your eyes and come back into the room.

Some Guidelines for How to Interpret Your Journey

We are asked to land in a place we have never visited before to ensure it is a place entirely created by our imaginations. The geographical terrain we land in may reflect our current internal state of mind, as outer terrain can reflect our inner terrain. How useful and pertinent to our situation the items we have with us are can mirror how well equipped we feel to deal with life. Being able to make a pathway symbolizes our capacity to make headway in life. How able we are to stake a claim to something that belongs to us may reflect how able we are to claim what is our due in life. This part of the journey puts us in touch with the "conquering hero" aspect of Mars. How at ease we are with this can show how able we are to assert ourselves. In the journey, are we able to defend our territory? How do we fight, and what are our weapons? All this symbolizes how able we are to defend ourselves and fight for our corner in the other, more subtle domains of life.

Symbolically, the sword represents Mars. The condition of the sword, what it is like, where it is found, what surrounds it, what use it is, and whether or not we keep it will reveal something of how this principle is operating.

On a different level, the sword can also be seen as a phallic symbol. It may mirror how a man feels about his penis and all that his penis represents to him in relation to his masculinity, and how a woman feels about her own metaphorical penis and her masculine side. It may also reveal more literally how a woman feels about a man's penis.

How difficult or passive the rival is may show the extent of our fear and threat of others in life. Our rival often has qualities that are unacknowledged and disliked parts of ourselves, and these are what binds us to an enemy. How we deal with our rival may reveal how we relate to disowned and disliked aspects of ourselves, as well as how effective we can be when challenged.

The decision we have to make may be either an imaginary decision that is within the context of the guided imagery journey or a real-life decision we are facing. If it's the latter, then this is the time to focus on it. When it is an entirely imaginary decision, the journey may still cast light on how we deal with real-life decisions or arrive at decisions.

Next we look at some of the qualities that we find attractive in others, and at how comfortable or uncomfortable we are with our feelings of sexual attraction. We would expect that our chart would describe the person we feel sexually attracted to. Those we find sexually attractive often have qualities that are unacknowledged and liked parts of ourselves, and these are what bind us to a lover. Whereas our rival receives our disowned negative attributes, our lover will tend to receive the disowned positive ones (although not necessarily).

For those of us unable either to acknowledge or communicate our attraction, there may be problems in life in establishing a relationship with someone of our choice. Maybe we do not enter into relationships, or we play passive roles in our relationships, allowing ourselves to be chosen rather than exercising our choice. This could leave us feeling a lack of commitment to our partner—we are not really taking responsibility for our involvement.

Dancing has a sexual component and is another form of physical activity that involves relating. How involved or separated we are when dancing may reveal attitudes we have toward "togetherness" and "separateness," and toward shared activity in general. Maybe we cannot accept our sexual feelings. Many of us have deep-seated guilt around sexuality which can cripple us emotionally. For all of us who have difficulties in this area, this part of the guided imagery journey will illuminate what our difficulties are, which is the first step toward being able to do something about them.

Bravery is the next dimension of Mars' principle that we look at. The ways we are brave will vary with our individual Mars placement. Some of us may not be aware of what constitutes bravery for us. We often have very stereotypical ideas of what being brave or courageous means. Being brave simple consists of doing anything we are afraid to do. Even if there is no recognition from others that we have been brave, it is important that at least *we* recognize when we have dared to do something that is difficult for us and give ourselves credit.

The final part of the journey explores our competitive spirit. Theoretically, competition stretches us to achieve our individual best, and achieving our best brings satisfaction. So, provided we have achieved our personal best, we don't mind if we are beaten by someone else. This requires knowing what our best is and having some sense of our own limits. Clearly, this is an ideal that many of us fail to reach. Watch to see how you feel in the competitive situation in the imagery.

In order to compete, we have to be able to lose. If we can't afford emotionally to lose, we can't take the risk and compete at all, which will have a severely limiting effect on us. Some of us may find the competitive side of ourselves so difficult that we avoid obvious competitive situations entirely. Yet we do all compete in life on some level, just to get on and survive. Even when apparently cooperating or being altruistic we have our own personal agenda. If we can't openly compete, we disguise it, and we could be said to be less honest.

Other People's Journeys

Let us go on to look at the charts and journeys of a woman and a man who took this journey with me on May 15, 1993 and April 19, 1996, respectively. The accounts are reproduced here verbatim, as they were recorded at the time. Retrospectively, as we become detached from the emotional experience of the guided imagery journey, we have more insight, and my comments and interpretation benefit from this. Where I have made connections back to the participant's natal chart I have inserted the astrological signifiers in parentheses in their text.

"In my parachute I land in quite a barren place; it is as though there had once been some large buildings, maybe an industrial estate, which had all been demolished and the stone and brick carted away. (Mars square Uranus) To the right, at a little distance, is quite a dark forest. (Moon conjunct Mars) In the distance ahead I can see some houses and hear sounds of habitation, but these seem a long way away. I have some string bags hanging at my waist in which there is some food (Moon conjunct Mars), a knife (Mars), some toy wooden bricks (Mars trine Saturn), and a thermos flask of water. (Moon in Pisces) I don't see much of a path, just stony ground covered in debris. (Mars trine Saturn, Mars square Uranus) The land is gently undulating.

"I decide that how I am going to mark this land as mine is by beating the bounds and putting up a fence, but this fence is purely symbolic as anyone could climb over it. It is only knee high. (Mars trine Saturn, Mars opposite Jupiter) I am not sure how I will protect my land, as I feel any danger will come from the air. This has a space-age feel to it, something alien that I feel quite uncomfortable with. (Mars square Uranus)

"As I walk into the woods, I find the sword lying on the ground. It is quite short and fat, heavy, encrusted with red and green jewels. (Moon conjunct Mars in Pisces) It isn't new or sharp, but has been well cared for. It seems to have a protective function rather than be a fighting weapon. (Moon conjunct Mars) I meet my rival. He is standing in my path, arms folded across his chest. He is tall, dressed in a long, hooded, grey robe. He has red eyes and long grey hair. (Mars trine Saturn) Even when I tell him I will just have to go around him, he doesn't move. I decide to ask him to leave, and he does so. (Mars square Uranus) I find a large rock to rest on and consider the decision to be made. (This bit I forgot about at first when I wrote up the notes.) This decision is about whether to leave this land or to remain here, and I feel I have to weigh up the pros and cons before I can come to a real decision, so I leave it for the moment and go on walking through the forest. It feels as though it has to do with moving house. (Moon conjunct Mars, square Uranus)

"Then I meet the man I find sexually attractive. He is dressed in green and brown soft suede, a Robin Hood type character. He is busy chopping wood. There is an easygoing feel to him that I like, unruffled, laughing. He is brown skinned, looks fit and healthy. (Mars in Pisces opposite Jupiter, Mars trine Saturn in Cancer) I feel my heart jump and try to be vivacious so he will notice me. (Mars semisquare Venus) But I feel the attraction is more that of a kindred spirit than a purely sexual one. (Moon conjunct Mars, Neptune conjunct the MC) Pan pipes start to play in the distance and we dance. Sometimes we hold each other close, at other times it seems a sort of courtly dance. (Venus in Aries rules MC, Neptune conjunct MC, Mars semisquare Venus, Mars trine Saturn)

"Then a group of people arrive, laughing and talking. There is a big campfire, and the courageous task I have to perform is to dance through the fire. (Mars opposite Jupiter, stellium in Aries) This doesn't seem too difficult, and it is just my dress that is a bit singed at the end. When I landed in my parachute, I had been dressed in some kind of jumpsuit. (Venus in Aries)

"Now I have a simple peasant dress. The game we play is jumping over a high wire. (Mars opposite Jupiter) I don't win, don't jump the highest, but I jump well and feel I have done my best, and that seems to satisfy me. (Sun in Aries) Then it is time to go back to the parachute. I take the sword with me."

See Jill's chart on page 30. The place Jill lands in is barren and seems to represent the aftermath of the major transits to her Aries Sun occurring prior to her journey. (Transiting Uranus and Neptune squaring her Sun) She is in a state of transition, waiting for a new phase of life to emerge after the existing structures of her life have been demolished.

The dark forest symbolizes a rich inner life, and is signified by Jill's Moon Mars conjunction in Pisces. She is well prepared, apart from the toy wooden bricks, which perhaps symbolize a mischievous part of her psyche or her inability to actually put things right. These may relate to the need to rebuild parts of her life in the wake of the recent transits to her Sun. The stony ground and lack of a path, also echo this theme; she does not yet know where she is going.

Jill does not know how to protect her land, as she feels any danger will come from the air. She says this has an alien, space-age feel to it. Uranus immediately comes to mind, and in Jill's chart Uranus is not only conjunct the Descendent, but is square to the Moon and Mars. Jill is likely to project her Uranus onto others, and this part of her journey vividly describes her doing this.

The sword constellates Jill's Moon conjunct Mars, in that it is well cared for and has a protective function. It is encrusted with jewels, which perhaps shows a measure of how much Jill values her "inner penis." Her Sun in Aries conjunct Venus also comes to mind here, as a signifier of a valued masculine spirit. She also keeps her sword, so it can be seen as an integrated and internalized part of her psyche.

Jill's rival is male, so will be signified by masculine planets. His posture, clothing, and air of authority are typically Saturnian. His red eyes have to be signified by Mars, the red planet, the planet of anger, which is trine to Saturn. Initially, Jill is insufficiently assertive, and her rival stands his ground, signified by Mars and Saturn being placed in the water signs, but she then musters up enough strength to get him to leave, signified by the square from Mars to Uranus. This is not Jill's easiest option, but if pushed, she has it in her. Her rival can also be seen as an aspect of her inner masculine side, which will cave in when strongly challenged.

Jill's decision, which she realizes has to do with a real dilemma in her life—whether or not to move house—is signified by the Uranus and Neptune transits squaring her fourth house Sun. It is a common experience with these transits to feel in limbo, unable to make a decision, and whereas some of us get anxious and try to force a decision prematurely, Jill is able to allow her decision to wait.

The man she finds sexually attractive is an earthy/watery type signified by Mars in Pisces trine Saturn in Cancer and opposite Jupiter in Virgo. His relaxed manner, health, and vitality are signified by Jill's Mars Jupiter opposition, as is the Robin Hood character, a man who had his own brand of morality. Jill's response to him is pure Venus in Aries; she tries to attract his attention by being vivacious! Jill's feeling that the attraction is that of kindred spirits takes us back to her Moon Mars conjunction in Pisces, which longs for oneness, merging, and transcendence and may sublimate earthly desire. This is further accentuated by Neptune in Libra on the MC. The dance has a romantic and intimate feel, signified by Jill's Pisces planets, Neptune in Libra on the MC, and Venus Mars mutual reception, while Saturn and Uranus in the seventh house signify the formality of a courtly dance and the ambivalence of holding her partner at arms' length. So we have many mixed messages here. We have the desire for transcendence and intimacy combining with a need for formality with a hint of ambivalence.

Jill changes her attire to a more traditionally feminine form when sexuality is introduced, something other women have done, and we will discuss this at the end of this chapter. Her test of courage is to pass through fire, a symbol of transformation and regeneration. Fire is also associated with purification and spiritual strength, and Jill's test could represent her desire to transcend the human condition. That Jill is then unable to jump the highest seems to show that she is bound by the limits of her body. Yet she is satisfied, as she has done her best, so she seems to have accepted the limits of the human condition.

LANCE'S MARS JOURNEY

"I landed in a dry and dusty place. Behind lay mountains, ahead a rocky escarpment. I had seen a river in that direction and decided to go that way.

"I checked my supplies and equipment—including food, knife, change of clothing, lighter, picture of my son, compass—and traveled down the rocky path. To claim the land, I will live by the river I saw. I'll build a house there, and to defend myself, the river will naturally defend one side and the rocks the other, but I'll move some rocks and build a wall. (Mars in Taurus on the IC)

"As I scrambled over rocks, I saw something glitter. I looked closer and it was a sword. The sword was battered, but the blade was still sharp, and there were gems in the hilt. Some of them were missing. It used to be beautiful. I will use the sword to defend myself, to cut down trees, to skin animals, to dig, to carve. I picked it up and continued down the stony track. (Mars in Taurus on the IC)

"I saw a man coming towards me. He was a giant, black-haired and black-eyed. He was very pale. His eyes, face, and posture showed that he wanted to intimidate me, make me scared. (Sun conjunct Mars)

"I stopped walking and returned his stare. My hand moved to the hilt of the sword I'd found. I did not move until he had passed by. (Mars opposite Neptune)

"I stop to rest by the river. I'm sitting on a smooth boulder. Across the river is a forest full of powerful trees. (Sun conjunct Mars on the IC, Moon conjunct Saturn in Pisces)

"I decide to build my house on this spot and once built, I'll stop wandering, I'll be stable. If I finish it. (Sun conjunct Mars in Taurus on the IC, opposite Neptune)

"I decide I want to build my beautiful house. (Sun conjunct Mars in Taurus on the IC)

"I move on, cross the river, and I'm entering the forest borders. I see a woman. She's dark-haired, dark-eyed, dark-skinned. She's glowing with health. She looks totally natural, athletic, voluptuous. (Mars and Venus in mutual reception) She looks at peace with herself and her world. That attracts me. (Mars opposite Neptune, Moon in Pisces) I feel as though I need to know her, so I smile into her eyes. She responds by smiling back.

"We both hear some Latin/Brazilian-type music drifting out of the forest. We dance. The dance is wild, free, and uninhibited. It makes me feel alive.

"A group of people come. They listen to my plans concerning the home I want to build. One of them challenges me to build it within a specified time. I build it. Some think I'm brave, some don't see why I consider it to be a big deal.

"Someone suggests we play tennis. I play hard to win, but I lose. I don't feel badly about losing because it's just a game. (Sun conjunct Mars opposite Neptune)

"I wander back through my land, and when I come to the place where I found my sword, I put it back. It may help another traveler." (Neptune on the MC)

See Lance's chart on page 32. Lance lands exceptionally well equipped. Not only does he have items that are associated with survival, but he has thought of his comfort and emotional relationships; he has a change of clothes and picture of his son. He demonstrates here the practicality and resourcefulness of Taurus.

To claim the land, Lance builds a house on it, a delightful illustration of Mars in Taurus on the IC. He is using his physical energy (Mars) in a constructive way (Taurus) to build a home (the IC). He is providing himself with a secure base, perhaps concretizing something he has on an inner level. He makes use of the natural resources to defend his territory, reflecting his ability to be in tune with nature and use it to his own advantage.

The sword Lance finds is battered, with some of its gems missing, perhaps reflecting his experiences of struggle and loss. The sword is still sharp, suggesting he has not suffered serious loss, he has not been diminished. Lance has a number of uses for his sword, illustrating a healthy survival instinct. Carving is one of the uses which shows creativity.

Creativity is signified astrologically in a number of ways in Lance's chart. He has an aspect pattern called a mystic rectangle that relates to creative potential involving the Sun, Moon, Mars, Saturn, Uranus, Neptune, Pluto, and the MC/IC axis. This is quite an exceptional pattern, and involving, as it does, most of Lance's chart, it is central to him. More specifically, Lance has the Sun, the creative heart of the chart, conjunct Mars in Taurus, a sign associated with the more tactile forms of artistic expression. They are on the IC, the most private point in the chart, indicating creativity and originality expressed in tangible, physical ways. Neptune opposes the Sun and Mars, adding an imaginative and sensitive flair to the way he does things.

Lance manifests his Mars Neptune opposition in another way when he meets his rival. Lance meets his stare, stands his ground, is passive and contained, yet exudes a strength. He conveys clearly that he is capable of defending himself and finds he does not have to use aggression; instead, he outwits his rival. This has strong parallels with the animal kingdom, in which males jockey for dominance. Violence erupts only when an animal fails to recognize its place within the hierarchy and refuses to be submissive. In Lance's case, his rival decides not to take him on. He recognizes he has met his match and that a fight would be unwise. This indicates that Lance feels capable of holding his own in life, even against a giant. This rather menacing figure is also a shadow side of himself, a side he does not identify with.

The river and the forest full of powerful trees can be seen as metaphors for Lance's emotional and instinctive sexual nature. He meets a woman he is attracted to just as he enters the forest, as he crosses the threshold. Here he enters his deeper feelings, connecting to a more primitive, archaic side of himself. She embodies the qualities of Mars and Venus found in mutual reception (in each other's signs), and represents a part of Lance that he needs to unite with: his inner feminine qualities. The music is a sensual part of him that is vibrant and alive. The flavor of Lance's imagery reflects his sensitivity and strong, feeling nature. With the Sun in Taurus on the IC, he is rooted in something very creative and feminine.

Lance's challenge seems very ordinary, very achievable. He does not appear to have any hostile internal objects. Nothing terrible is going to happen to him if he does not complete his task, and nobody is really critical of him. He is self-accepting. He does, in fact, achieve his main aim, which is to build his house within a specified time, but he goes on to lose his game of tennis. The game acts as a metaphor for his competitive spirit in life, and one has to question why he imagines himself losing. Lance rationalizes his loss as unimportant, dismissing it as only a game. Neptune may be at work here, with its slippery, elusive quality. While his Taurean side may genuinely be as relaxed as he says he is about losing, this could also indicate superb Neptunian defenses at work that deflect any feelings he may have about losing.

Lance returns to the theme of his house, a central motif, many times on the guided imagery journey. His Sun in Taurus on the IC signifies his need to have a home and settle down. He craves stability, a quality he has within but which, with Neptune so strongly placed in his chart, can also elude him. His home represents a bedrock of inner security, a tangible externalized expression of his soul.

Several of the women who have been on this journey have taken on a masculine identity. It is as if they cannot express their Mars energy as women, so they adopt a male body. Those who retain their female identity often dress in traditionally male clothing. However, when they get to the part of the journey where they meet someone they find sexually attractive, the women revert back to a female body and don classic female attire. It seems that sexuality is the expression of Mars that women can most readily accept and identify with. Other expressions of Mars seem to require that they emulate masculine characteristics. The women I have worked with have all been heterosexual, and while I must not generalize too much from a small sample, it would be interesting to see what differences, if any, lesbian women have in terms of their gender identification when expressing Mars principle.

From these journeys we can see that the whole chart needs to be considered when understanding how Mars' principle is expressed. One woman
with Mars in Virgo, a practical, efficient, and humble sign, was ferocious.
Mars was in the first house, which signified, along with other chart factors,
the extent to which she found the world a threatening place, and as a consequence she responded with fierceness herself. Virgo is not in itself a fierce
sign, but one of service, and this woman enlisted Mars' service in protecting
her from perceived threats. This emphasizes that the whole chart and the
house position of Mars are of paramount importance in understanding your
journey.

CHAPTER 7

Jupiter

♃

Jupiter represents the principle of expansion. It urges us to extend ourselves, to stretch, to attempt more, to better ourselves. Jupiter represents a part of us that is searching. At its best, this search is for knowledge and wisdom. Jupiter is concerned with moral and ethical issues that effect all of us in society. Jupiter has to do with conscience. Someone with a strong Jupiter may set a high moral tone, but could have their own idiosyncratic morality, not necessarily in accord with society's. Jupiter is a philosophical and religious planet. It is concerned with the meaning of things and urges us towards greater understanding. In the search for greater understanding we feel the urge to explore, to travel physically, mentally, and spiritually beyond our usual horizons.

This sounds very positive, but the urge to expand can also be negative, if we are never satisfied with what we have. Our consumer society relies on Jupiter's principle to fuel our appetite for more. Our belief that the grass is going to be greener over the hill comes from Jupiter. So, Jupiter's principle can feed a feeling of restlessness and dissatisfaction with what we have. Jupiter and Saturn together create a balance between expansion and limitations, but by itself Jupiter urges us to expand without limits, to proliferate.

Jupiter is traditionally known as the greater benefic, a planet whose influence is considered benign. It is associated with good fortune and luck, without any closer inspection of why this is so. Jupiterean good luck often expresses itself in our ability to recognize an opportunity and seize it, to see future potential in something. It may or may not bear fruit, but because of the nature of Jupiter, we tend to bounce back from failure very quickly, dust ourselves off, and start all over again. Someone with a strong Jupiter will tend to be generous, and that generosity will come back in the form of good will and other benefits.

Jupiter's principle infuses us with hope and faith in life, ourselves, and others. Our faith may or may not be justified, but Jupiter fuels our innate optimism. Jupiter sees the bottle half full, and Saturn sees it half empty. Both are right. Depending on the relative strengths of these two planets within our chart, we will tend to slant in one direction or the other, although some of us will seesaw between an optimistic and a pessimistic outlook on life. If, as some believe, we create our own reality by what we believe, then if we have a strong Jupiter and accordingly an optimistic outlook, we will generate good fortune for ourselves. At least this is how we will perceive things.

Jupiter and Saturn are both associated with "the teacher" archetype, but, depending on whether Jupiter or Saturn is stronger in our chart, the way we learn and the kind of teacher we become will be, in fact, very different. With Saturn we learn from life's hard knocks and become wise and expert through facing our difficulties. With Jupiter we are inspired, we have a thirst to know, and knowledge is revealed to us. Jupiterian teachers inspire and enthuse others, so they too set out on the quest of discovery.

Our Jovian side will always have a tendency to exaggerate, to see things in a positive light, and to make light of difficulties. When given too free a reign, and when coupled with unacknowledged psychological wounding, this can lead to arrogance, grandiosity, inflation, and omnipotence. Jupiter, when compensating for perceived inner lacks, will go right over the top in the most spectacular ways. Arrogance is a Jupiterean way of covering up insecurity and self-doubt. Grandiosity is the next level, at which a person's sense of self is so seriously wounded that she or he permanently adopt an attitude that overestimates self-worth and value. Such a person may impress those who are similarly wounded and caught up in the same dynamic, but not those who can see through the subterfuge.

Inflation occurs when we lose contact with our humanness and ordinariness and become identified with something archetypal, something god-like outside ourselves. We lose contact with our own fallibility and mortality. Those caught up in grandiosity and inflation may live in dread of being discovered to be a sham. It is ultimately debilitating to try to bluff your way through things, knowing somewhere inside that you can not fulfill your promise.

Omnipotence is a defense strategy adopted by some who have suffered early psychological wounding, whereby they believe they have ultimate control and act as if they were invulnerable. The trouble with all these defensive measures is that they continue to perpetuate the wound rather than heal it.

My emphasis on some of the problems associated with Jupiter's principle is to adjust the balance, as Jupiter has been given such good press over the years. Jupiter does create a feel-good factor, so when we are under its influence, even when caught up in its more negative manifestations, we tend to feel fine (as opposed to when we are under Saturn's influence). We say someone has gone "O.T.T.," over the top, referring to an unrestrained expression of Jupiter's principle. Jupiter's principle has gotten out of hand if, for example, we are staving off bankruptcy but believe we are in funds, or if we are verging on obesity yet have no diagnosed medical problem. In both scenarios we are out of control, and Jupiter's principle is running amok. (Financial problems and weight problems have, by no means, only to do with Jupiter's principle. Venus is associated with money as well as pleasure and sensuality, and the Moon describes our ability to nurture ourselves. So either of these planetary principles may also be implicated where there are financial and weight problems.)

Jupiter's principle is freedom orientated, encouraging us to be free to realize our full potential and resist any restrictions. Jupiter's principle urges us to travel, study, and think deeply about things of ultimate concern. Zeus, the Greek god associated with Jupiter, was the king of the gods. Jupiter is in many ways a king of a planet, but Jupiter's domain is a lot less personal than that of the Sun.

In the guided imagery that follows, various symbolic scenarios are presented which put us in touch with Jupiter's principle, so we may see how this principle operates within us. Before you begin this journey, please refer to *Some Guidelines Before Going on a Guided Imagery Journey* in Chapter 1 and go through the *Relaxation Exercise* given there.

Guided Imagery Journey on Jupiter's Principle

— I want you to imagine you are someone of noble blood in days gone by. (short pause)

— You are also an adventurer. (short pause)

— You ride a horse. (pause)

— You particularly enjoy galloping into the wind across wild, open spaces. (short pause)

— You love the speed. (pause)

— Your favorite ride is along a deserted beach that runs for miles. (short pause)

— The sand is firm. You give your horse his head, and he virtually flies along, the water stretching out for miles on one side and uninhabited countryside on the other. (pause)

— You feel exhilarated and uplifted. (short pause)

— Eventually your horse slows down to a steady trot. (short pause)

— There's a special place where you sometimes stop. (short pause)

— You let your horse roam, and you sit on a particular rock and gaze out into the distance. (pause)

— You are moved to contemplate various issues that never fail to fascinate and intrigue you. (short pause)

— Your mind is restless, seeking to discover a new understanding, stretching out to grasp something right on the edge of your understanding. (short pause)

— Let your mind travel now to ideas you barely comprehend yet want to grasp and know better. (long pause)

— What do you want to learn more about? (pause)

— In what ways do you want to grow? (pause)

— In what way do you seek to reach out farthest? (pause)

— Focus now on the issue of freedom. (short pause)

— How do you long to be free? (pause)

— Where do you seek the most freedom? (pause)

— You call your horse and remount. (short pause)

— You are going to visit someone whose counsel always inspires you. This is an imaginary person. (short pause)

— Notice the way to this person's abode (short pause), and be aware of any questions you want to ask. (pause)

— When you arrive, you enter (short pause) and sit together in silence for a short time. (pause)

— When you are ready, ask the questions that have been forming in your mind. (pause)

— Hear their reply. (pause)

— You then say good-bye and leave (short pause), returning on your horse (short pause) past your favorite rock (short pause) along the deserted beach (short pause) to where you set out from.

When you are ready, open your eyes and come back into the room.

Some Guidelines for How to Interpret Your Journey

Participants are asked to imagine themselves as someone of noble blood in days gone by in order to introduce Jupiter's majestic, royal quality. Some participants imagine an actual person, rather than an imaginary one. Our associations to a real person are significant and should be explored afterwards. Through an identification with someone of noble blood (real or otherwise), we get in touch with our own feelings of grandeur and stature.

Horses are traditionally associated with Jupiter and contribute to the atmosphere of the journey. Even those who have never ridden, or are generally nervous of horses, usually get swept along by the guided imagery and put their fears behind them.

In this first part of the journey, we are building upon a positive experience to create a feeling of expansiveness. Participants generally have a feeling of well-being conjured by the landscape and by traveling at speed in a wide open space. This feeling of well-being is important because it sets the tone for the next part of the journey. Exhilarated and uplifted we can turn our minds to other dimensions.

We are asked to stretch our minds, to reach towards things we are struggling to understand. Though it's difficult to get hold of things just out of our mind's grasp, what is important is the act of stretching. We may not have a lot to report on at this point, but we have identified a process and can return to it at other times. Mental exercise is as important as physical exercise; like the muscles of our body, our minds atrophy if we do not stretch them and use them. Many of us recognize that after periods of not having to think, our minds become "rusty" and take a while to get going.

Next, we are asked to look specifically at ways we would like to expand. The answers that emerge, when they do, provide us with a wealth of information about what is important for us in our future personal growth. Our answers will show us in what ways we need to be free. This information will reflect Jupiter's placement in our chart and can provide us a foundation for future plans. If our answers are incomplete, we can always return to the questions. Exploring our thoughts enlivens the mind and leaves us feeling mentally uplifted.

The next part of the journey puts us in touch with our inner wise counselor. This counselor is an inspired part of ourselves, in touch with a bigger truth. Struggling to answer the questions we've just posed will have already brought up this aspect of ourselves. Now we are making the connection more concrete.

The way to the person's house is not necessarily significant in terms of Jupiter, but it does provide an important transition during which one can digest the just-finished part of the journey and prepare oneself for the next stage. Our description of our inspired counselor reflects the inspired part of ourselves. The new questions we now form will tend to be similar to the questions we have just been grappling with, but they will be even more personal.

A deep communion between you and the counselor is established by sitting in silence together, circumventing social niceties. We are given an opportunity to go straight to the heart of issues that matter to us. We are with someone with whom we have a deep rapport. Our questions and their answers, which of course come from a wise and inspired part of ourselves, may surprise us. What is most important at this stage is connecting to this part of ourselves, the wise inner counselor, whom we can turn to whenever we need real guidance.

Other People's Journeys

Let's go on to look at the charts and journeys of two women I led through this journey on June 5, 1993. The accounts reproduced here are as they were written by them at the time. Where I have made connections back to their natal chart, I have inserted the astrological signifiers in parentheses in their text.

OLIVIA'S JUPITER JOURNEY

"I am a Lady, like Guinevere, at the court of King Arthur. There are lots of knights in shining armor. (Mars Saturn conjunction in Libra)

"Then I'm in a French court in the sixteen or seventeen-hundreds. I'm on a horse and my long hair is streaming behind me as we canter along. The scenery is very bleak and rugged with storm clouds. The atmosphere is rugged—it's like I'm Cathy looking for Heathcliffe. (Moon in Libra opposite Jupiter)

"I stop at a rock and look far out to the sea. I want to eat, and a large plate of liver and bacon arrives. I eat hungrily—it's gorgeous. Plates of steaming food keep arriving until I just can't eat anymore. (Moon opposite Jupiter)

"I want to grow by understanding my fears, to be strong, brave, and happy. (Jupiter opposite Mars and Saturn) When I think about freedom, I twirl round and round with my arms open and it feels really good. I want space and freedom. There are people just outside my arm span, but I won't let them in. I feel free and liberated as I twirl around—no responsibilities, just feeling carefree. (Jupiter in Aries in the third) Then, after a while, I drop my arms a bit and allow them to come closer, because I start to feel lonely. (Moon conjunct Saturn)

"I go off to see the wise man. He's a very old man with a long beard. (Mars conjunct Saturn in the ninth) He lives in a cave and walks with a staff. There are animals around him and Mimi, my cat who died, is there with him. (Mercury, ruler of the sixth, in Sagittarius in the twelfth)

"I asked him for help and to give me advice about what to do in the future. I asked him to help me find some meaning amidst this confusion.

"He said I needed faith and belief, and if I searched, I would find it. (Jupiter in Aries, stellium in the ninth, Sun and Mercury conjunct Sagittarius Ascendant)

"I felt unsure and rather dissatisfied. It all seemed so vague, just words. (Moon conjunct Saturn, Neptune in the ninth) There's a big gap. I come riding back along the beach."

See page 34 for Olivia's chart. Olivia starts her journey as a Lady, like Guinevere, and then she settles for being in the French court of the seventeenth or eighteenth century. Perhaps this change demonstrates the Libran propensity to vacillate. She has the Moon, Mars, Saturn, Neptune, and MC in Libra. The knights in shining armor can be seen as an embodiment of her

Mars Saturn conjunction, Mars symbolizing war, Saturn the rigidity and defensiveness of armor, and Libra the sign of courtliness.

Olivia has long hair streaming behind her as she canters along on her horse. The wind in her hair evokes the feeling of freedom that this journey engenders. The landscape is bleak with storm clouds, and the atmosphere is rugged, which may reflect her emotional landscape. She likens herself to Cathy looking for Heathcliffe, looking for an ideal perfect love, a soul mate. This is part of the emotional landscape as well. We might expect relationship issues to be on the agenda with Jupiter opposite the Moon in Libra, the sign associated with relationships.

Olivia wants to eat. A large plate of liver and bacon arrives, and food keeps on arriving until she can't eat anymore. Nurture is symbolized by the Moon, and the plentifulness is shown by its opposition to Jupiter. This reflects that Olivia is quite confident of getting her needs met.

When sitting on the rock in contemplation, Olivia recognizes that she wants to understand her fears, to be strong, brave, and happy. She gives us a delightful illustration of the influence of Jupiter, the planet associated with greater understanding, in opposition to Saturn, the planet associated with our fears, and Mars, the planet associated with being strong and brave. She demonstrates here a creative resolution to these opposing energies.

Olivia experiences freedom in a physical way; she twirls around with her arms open, keeping others literally at arms' length. This reflects her ability to keep people at arms' length in her life when necessary. She is very open emotionally and demonstrates the childlike innocence of Jupiter in Aries in the third house, the house of short journeys and the immediate environment. Later she chooses to allow others to come closer. First, she illustrates Moon Jupiter in her need for space and freedom, then moves on to Moon Saturn, which is susceptible to feeling lonely. She is aware of her different needs and the different sides of herself.

Olivia's wise man is an inner paternal figure, a benign manifestation of the Mars Saturn conjunction in the ninth house. He obviously takes care of animals, and her cat, who has died, is with him. Perhaps this is a figure who looks after the spirits of those who have passed away. In Olivia's chart,

Mercury, the ruler of the sixth house, the house of pets, is in Sagittarius in the twelfth house, the house associated with the spiritual realm. That her cat, with whom she had a close emotional bond, should be here is truly an affirmation of her beliefs.

Olivia asks him to help her find meaning amidst her confusion. The wise man tells her it is there for her to find. Meaning is within her and within her grasp. Olivia also asks him to give her advice regarding the future, to which he replies that she needs faith and belief. Olivia remains unconvinced; she is struggling to trust what she in fact already knows. The struggle within her between faith and doubt is signified by Jupiter and Saturn, which oppose each other.

Olivia's journey ends on a note of doubt, although her journey has been joyful. Jupiter is the ruler of Olivia's chart. She has the Sun and Mercury in Sagittarius, the sign Jupiter rules, as well as a stellium in the ninth house, which resonates with Jupiter, so we would expect this journey to be of particular significance for her. She is left trying to reconcile the gap, the divide within her between having tremendous innate faith and belief and a more doubtful, skeptical side which wants something more concrete to rely on. Yet doubt fuels the impetus to know more; if we are too sure we crystallize and become closed. Olivia demonstrates a fluctuating balance between Jupiter and Saturn's principle, which can take her forward in life.

ANN'S JUPITER JOURNEY

"At first I was Cardinal Richelieu in red robes. Then, when you said adventurer, I became Christopher Columbus in armor—no helmet— riding my brown horse through forest trees and fields. (Jupiter in Capricorn, Sun in Scorpio conjunct IC)

"When on a beach—white sand, horse became white—and we rode together, I was now the same youth in armor from the solar journey, though still Christopher Columbus. My favorite spot was a cove like Lulworth. (Sun in Scorpio on the IC) I let horse roam and sat on a rock and thought about why I was here. But I knew the answer. I was here to learn and grow and be prepared for the next journey. (Sun in Scorpio, Jupiter in Capricorn)

"I wanted to know why the world was such a mess, and I wanted to come to grips with relationships and my mother, wanted to know what had made her the way she was. (Sun square Moon)

"Freedom—when on rock took off armor—cartwheeled on beach in undergarments—gamboled and danced—paddled and splashed in water. Then had to put on armor to ride horse—saddled, not bareback. (Jupiter in Capricorn, rules fifth house)

"Didn't understand. Where did I want freedom? I was already experiencing it here in my favorite place, where I was safe. (Sun in Scorpio on IC, Jupiter in Capricorn)

"I climbed on my horse, and we climbed a sheer cliff path and rocks—horse very sure-footed—reached top—(Jupiter in Capricorn) clear path to slate cottage—smoke coming out of chimney—wasn't sure who would be there—the old woman or Merlin—when I went in it was the old woman—sitting in a high-back wooden chair—like a witch—cauldron on fire, not lit, dark—only natural light through small windows. I sat on only other chair—small table between us. I asked, Why were people not learning and growing as they should, but constantly repeating own mistakes? (Sun in Scorpio on IC)

"Answer: People had to make mistakes to learn—but yes it was true—things weren't right—people had lost touch with their spirituality and this was having a bad effect. (Sun in Scorpio on IC, Jupiter in Capricorn)

"I asked, Why did I hate my mother? Answer: Because she wants to own you and you can't be owned. (Sun in Scorpio on IC square Moon in Aquarius)

"I left and rode down the cliff as before—galloping past the rock and along the beach."

See Ann's chart on page 28. Ann changes gender again on this journey. She seems to become the same gender as the planetary principle; Jupiter represents a masculine principle and Ann becomes male. She starts her journey as Cardinal Richelieu, a ruthless French statesman of the seventeenth century, signified by Pluto rising and Mars in the first. He reflects a ruthless aspect of Ann.

Ann then becomes Christopher Columbus in armor, a great explorer, riding her horse through forest trees and fields. Forests can be seen to symbolize the feminine principle, the great mother, and the unconscious, so we could say Ann is exploring her unconscious, symbolized astrologically by the midnight Sun in Scorpio. Next, she becomes the same youth, in armor, that she was on her solar journey, as well as Christopher Columbus. She has a dual identity, but perhaps what is of importance here is that whatever identity she adopts, she still wears armor; she remains defended.

The cove is an enclosed, secure place, perhaps representative of the womb and signified by the Sun on the IC. Within this privacy and safety, Ann removes her armor, she lets down her defenses. Like Olivia, she experiences freedom in a physical way, cartwheeling on the beach in her undergarments, dancing, and splashing in the water. She has liberated herself from her restrictive armor and is enjoying her freedom. Jupiter is in Capricorn in Ann's chart, so perhaps this is why she experiences freedom in such a tangible form. Jupiter rules the fifth house, the house of creative self-expression, and Ann seems to be saying, "This is me." Something in Ann wants to be free of encumbrances, to be free of her defenses, to be herself. Later, it seems she is content with the fact that she can experience freedom when she feels safe, when she can let her defenses down at will.

Ann thinks about why she is here, and knows the answer immediately: She is here to learn and grow and prepare for the next journey. It's an expression of her Jupiter in Capricorn, learning through experience, and her Sun in Scorpio, an implicit belief in reincarnation. This is perhaps innate with the Sun on the IC in the sign associated with transformative process. Ann's life path is to grow in understanding through her instincts rather than through her intellect.

Ann wants to know why the world is such a mess. While there is no denying the relevance of her concern, this may also be a projection onto the world of her own inner state. Next comes Ann's concern about her relationship with her mother and how her mother became the way she was. We are back with the feminine principle and what has been passed down to Ann through the generations. Perhaps her concern about the state of the world and her mother have the same root.

Jupiter in Capricorn is apparent in the steep slope Ann's horse has to climb to get to the cottage, which sounds more like the kind of path a goat might take. This is also not an easy route to access her inner wise woman. The witchy old woman is a figure Ann has encountered before, and can be seen as an inner mother figure. The darkness of the cottage reflects difficulties, as does the small table between her and the old woman, which specifically represents an obstacle, a barrier between her and her wisdom, and also a barrier between her and her mother.

Ann asks the old woman why people were not learning and growing, why they were repeating their own mistakes. The reply she gets is partly reassuring: People have to make mistakes in order to learn. It seems as if Ann is concerned about the mistakes she feels she is making. This is signified by Jupiter in Saturn's sign of Capricorn.

Ann is told that people have lost touch with their spirituality and that this was having a bad effect. Perhaps Ann is concerned that she has lost touch with her own spirituality, and this is having a bad effect on her. Ann asks why she hates her mother and is told it's because her mother wants to own her and she can't be owned. Perhaps Ann's loss of spirituality is connected to hating her mother. Ann doesn't want to be controlled, but she controls herself by wearing her armor, and her internal mother (the witch) also controls her. The armor, representing her defenses, was put on in part to protect her from her mother, but now it shuts her off from herself and her connection to her inner feminine wisdom. As long as she is alienated from her mother, she is also alienated from her own spiritual source.

We see manifested in this journey the defensiveness of Pluto rising and the Sun in Scorpio on the IC, along with Ann's need to explore the rather threatening territory of the unconscious in order to tap into her powerful instinctual wisdom. Jupiter is also in a feminine sign, an earth sign, pointing the way toward this.

This journey has presented different dilemmas to these two participants. What is consistent for them, and for others who have been on this journey, are the feelings it leaves them with. Despite problems this Jupiter journey may reveal, it will nevertheless leave participants uplifted, in touch with Jupiter's expansive, exhilarating principle. For those feeling hemmed in by circumstances and wanting to experience a breath of fresh air in their lives, this is a good journey to go on. It will not disguise deep-seated issues you may need to deal with, but it can provide some relief, direction, and optimism.

CHAPTER 8

Saturn

ħ

Saturn symbolizes our personal limitations. Its placement shows our Achilles' heel, where we are vulnerable, what we will have to struggle with, and where, as a result of our struggle, we will become expert. Our Saturn placement, by sign, house, and aspect shows how and in what ways we are in pain—it shows our hurt. It shows where there is inner doubt and uncertainty, where we lack confidence and, as a result, may try to bolster ourselves. This is why this planet is so often hated and feared. We want to distance ourselves from the feelings of insecurity and inadequacy that Saturn's placement shows and do not take kindly to looking at the important lessons we are learning through grappling with "our issues." Saturn's placement shows where we most long to feel secure and where we are most defended.

As we mature, life deals us a certain number of hard knocks, and in coming to terms with our difficulties, we move towards developing the wise face of Saturn, the teacher from life experience. By midlife we are usually more able to accept our limitations and no longer rail against them as we did in our more idealistic youth, so Saturn's principle becomes more benign.

Saturn has to do with our innate desire for order and form, with the rules, knowing what they are and living within them. It is about adapting to live within society. Saturn is about things like self-discipline, duty, and responsibility, all of which we tend to find easier to manage as we mature. Someone with a strong Saturn will appear like a little old man or woman when young, with the burdens of the world on such young shoulders weighing them down. But come midlife, the load feels far lighter and easier to carry. So, from starting life old beyond their years, someone with a strong Saturn ages well and may feel positively sprightly by 50. Then, they can use their innate self-discipline and sense of responsibility in an appropriate way.

Saturn is the principle that enables us to get things done. We may have dreams, visions, and inspirational ideas, but without Saturn they remain in the world of potential. It takes Saturn to bring them into concrete reality. Saturn symbolizes the interface between us and society. The painter who never manages to put her work in front of the public, or the musician who only plays in his basement are having problems with Saturn's principle. A successful painter not only has to be able to paint, but to get her paintings framed and exhibited by a gallery. A musician to reach an audience has to get a recording contract.

If an artist's work does get out into the world, it is critiqued, another Saturn principle. Some would rather avoid this interface with the world, preferring never to know what others actually think of their work. If their Saturn is weak, they may not be able to get things together so that others can hear or see their creations. If Saturn is too strong, an individual may be so self-critical that their work never reaches a standard that they are happy with. But generally, Saturn's principle enables us to make things actually happen in the world, allows us to get things out there into the market place and be able to tolerate others' opinions.

Popular slogans of the mid-nineties, as Saturn moves through the poetic and chaotic sign of Pisces, are "Get a grip on reality" and "Get real." Here we see how Saturn's cycle influences society and how it can affect popular culture, as in advertising, for instance.

In the guided imagery that follows, various symbolic scenarios are presented that will put us in touch with Saturn's principle, so we may experience how this principle operates within us. Though Saturn signifies characteristics we tend to find difficult, on the whole, participants have not found this journey difficult or painful, as it is constructed to give us a positive experience of Saturn's principle. Anyone who ordinarily has difficulty with Saturn's principle could find this journey particularly helpful. Before you begin this journey, please refer to *Some Guidelines Before Going on a Guided Imagery Journey* in Chapter 1 and go through the *Relaxation Exercise* given there.

Guided Imagery Journey on Saturn's Principle

— I want you to imagine that you are a mole. (short pause)

— You're small and furry, and you live underground. (short pause)

— The earth around you is cool and damp and pleasant-smelling. (short pause)

— Be aware of its texture and consistency. (pause)

— You're digging a passage. (short pause)

— What is yours like? (pause)

— Is it straight? (short pause) Or bending? (short pause)

— Do you move quickly? (short pause) Or slowly? (short pause)

— What is your direction? (long pause)

— You come to a boulder. (short pause)

— It blocks your way forward. (short pause)

— How do you deal with this? (pause)

— Can you find a way forward and continue? (long pause)

— You are actually a part of a mole colony that has existed for thousands of years. (short pause)

— Imagine how you all relate as a colony now. (long pause)

— There are spoken and unspoken rules of how to behave and of what is acceptable. Imagine what they are. (long pause)

— There are even moles elected to uphold the spoken rules. (short pause)

— How do you fit in? (pause)

— How constrained do you feel by the rules? (pause)

— How protected do you feel by the rules? (pause)

— Do you betray anything of yourself to live in this colony? (pause)

— Within the colony is a very old and wise mole. (short pause)

— The mole has a home and you go to it. (pause)

— What does the mole look like? (pause)

— What is his or her home like? (pause)

— You can ask any question, and the mole will give you an answer. (short pause)

— Be aware of what you want to ask. (pause)

— Now ask your question. (short pause)

— And hear the mole's answer. (pause)

— You say good-bye and leave his or her home, coming back along the tunnel you've already made. (short pause)

— You go back to where you were in the beginning. (short pause)

When you are ready, open your eyes and gradually come back into the room.

Some Guidelines for How to Interpret Your Journey

An underground creature, the mole is used to conjure up a strong positive relationship to the earth and because a mole, quite literally, has to dig its own path through it. In this journey our progress depends on our own work and endeavor. How easy or difficult this is for us shows something of how Saturn's principle is operating. Some of us imagine heavy clay soil, which is very difficult to move through and requires slow, tedious work to get anywhere. Others have a light, loamy soil that they move through easily and effortlessly. We can recognize that this reflects how life feels for us.

Next, we look at our sense of direction, whether we know where we are heading and how directly we are heading for it, which will reflect our sense of motivation and direction in life. Saturn's principle has a lot to do with our sense of direction, our goals, our ambitions. Some of us may be bumbling along quite happily with no sense of direction, but if we are unhappy about not "getting somewhere" in life, we can at least attempt to see where our problem lies and try to remedy it.

Then comes the obstacle—a classic Saturnian phenomenon. How we deal with the obstacle in our imagery will reflect the intrinsic attitude we have towards obstacles, and may cast light on how we deal with them. Are we easily thwarted and defeated? Or are we challenged and spurred on by obstacles?

The size of our obstacle in the imagery is also relevant, reflecting how difficult we expect things to be. Some people imagine huge obstacles while others imagine small obstacles. Some find their obstacles very easy to get around, regardless of the actual size. They attack the problem with relish and energy, while others have difficulty with even a modest obstacle. What we imagine will reflect our innate attitude and our life experience. This can be seen as a chicken-and-egg situation: which comes first? Do we attract the kind of life experience that supports our innate attitude, or vice versa? Whatever the answer, it is clear that to anticipate that an obstacle will be overly difficult to surmount shows us to be pessimistic and defeatist, both negative qualities of Saturn.

How we get around our obstacle also has symbolic meaning. While this cannot be rigidly interpreted and depends on the individual, generally going around the obstacle to the left is a yin, feminine-based resolution, representing the use of the right brain, while going to the right represents using the left brain and a masculine, logical, rational approach. Going underneath the obstacle suggests digging down within oneself for solutions, possibly into one's psychological depths, while going over the boulder suggests going up into the intellect or spiritual realms for solutions. This is not to say there are not other creative and ingenious ways of dealing with obstacles. Someone with a Saturn Pluto aspect used magic to shrink her obstacle away. Someone with Saturn Uranus dynamited hers. The planetary symbolism of both these solutions speaks loudly.

The next part of the guided imagery reveals Saturn's principle within society: rules that make the wheels of social life run smoothly and protect us, yet can restrict and limit us as well. We explore here how well we fit into society, and at what price. The rules we imagine here are always revealing, as is the way we imagine life in the colony. Both speak to how adjusted we are in our larger society.

Some of us will always set ourselves outside of the norm of mainstream society. Some of us will kick against it. Our own natal Saturn may be in difficult aspect to other chart factors, making us therefore unable to internalize and incorporate its principle and likely to experience our Saturn as outside ourselves. The police, authorities, bureaucracies, and institutions all potentially receive negative Saturn projections and are perceived with hostility and fear. Consequently, these very aspects of society constrict and thwart us and will continue to do so until we are able to establish an inner reconciliation with this principle. The difficulty for those of us caught up in this way is probably rooted in our early relationship with our father, and often requires a fair amount of painful introspection to illuminate and heal.

Some of us are overattached to Saturn's principle, feeling very safe and comfortable within the rules, as if the rules represented some absolute truth. They do not; they are just an aspect of society's functioning that we have to be adjusted to in order to operate successfully within it. We can unduly restrict ourselves, which will block us from realizing other essential parts of ourselves. As a result, we will tend to have a hard time with the outer planets, which represent different aspects of truth and do not respect Saturnian reality at all.

The final part of the guided imagery connects us back to one of the most positive attributes of Saturn: the wise old man or woman who has the wisdom of experience. Some individuals see a clear connection to their father; others a special person; others to no one they recognize. Whoever it is we imagine, it will represent an aspect of ourselves that we can turn to. The home of our wise old mole will sometimes specifically describe the house placement of natal Saturn.

The question we ask of mole is always significant and will reflect our Saturn's placement. The question may be pertinent to our current situation, but usually it concerns some long-standing, deep-seated issue. Two things are important here: being able to formulate our question (as being able to name a problem is partway to solving it), and realizing that we hold the answer to the question within ourselves. Being able to access our inner wisdom is a valuable asset and a step toward genuine self-reliance.

Other People's Journeys

Let us now look at the charts and journeys of Michael and Olivia, who did this guided imagery journey in May, 1996 and on July 3, 1993, respectively. The accounts published here are as they were written by Michael and Olivia at the time. Where I have made connections back to their natal chart, I have inserted the astrological signifiers in parentheses in their text. This can be ignored by the nonastrologer. Their journeys are interpreted in the commentary that follows.

MICHAEL'S SATURN JOURNEY

"I am a mole digging away. The passage I am in has daylight at the end, and I am digging in the opposite direction. The clay is moist and crumbly and a bit pasty as I dig. There is a bit of a bend in the passageway, but you can still see the daylight. I realize I have to get rid of the soil as I dig. This is awkward: Do I have to go all the way back to the entrance with each bit I dig? Very tricky. (Saturn in Virgo)

"I come to the boulder. I start digging at the right-hand side, moving up in a semicircle around, looking for the nearest edge, which I eventually find on the left-hand side. I work my way around the boulder, and then my path seems to meander more, maybe because I can't see the daylight anymore. I don't know what direction I'm going in because I'm underground. I begin to wonder what's the point in digging this passage. I'm not trying to get to anywhere in particular, I'm just doing what I'm supposed to be doing. (Saturn semisextile Neptune)

"Elsewhere, there are tons of moles at work. They have little trucks and shovels and stand poring over maps and plans. (Saturn in Virgo) I'm not that interested—I don't really like it down here. Even though I don't smoke anymore, I feel like going up to the surface for a cigarette. It's night up there, and there's a huge yellow moon behind a bungalow. It's quiet and peaceful up here. (Mercury conjunct Neptune)

"Back down below, the moles are busy working and talking and gesticulating to each other without any reference to me. Nobody consults or informs me about what's going on. I feel a huge sadness. (Saturn in Virgo in the eighth, Uranus on the Descendant)

"I go along to the house of the old mole with tears in my eyes. I tell him I'm not really happy here as tears run down my cheeks. He just listens. His beard is so long it trails across the floor. His wife is busying herself doing things. The house is full of little knickknacks. (Saturn in Virgo) It's cozy, like an elf's house. I think that maybe I could live here with them and don't so much ask as suggest this. (Venus square Saturn) But then I look towards the back of the house and see a boy's bedroom and realize they already have someone living with them. Too bad. So I walk back along the tunnel to the daylight. It's a relief to get out of there."

See page 33 for Michael's chart. Michael starts his journey aware that he is moving away from daylight, away from the conscious level of life. In true Virgoan style he focuses on the practical problem of what to do with the earth, and is already beginning to feel taxed by the practical logistics of the task. The earth is easy to dig—he is not hampered in life—yet, despite this, he is dogged by the problem.

Michael initially attempts to dig around the boulder, going in the right direction, which indicates a more yang, rational, logical approach to problem solving, yet he keeps his options open and finds that the easiest way around is to go to the left, which represents using a more yin, intuitive, instinctive approach. What is interesting here is that he expects the logical approach to problems to work, but, in fact, his instincts serve him better.

Having successfully negotiated the boulder, Michael can no longer see daylight, and his path seems to meander more, perhaps reflecting that when he becomes less conscious of what he's doing, he loses his way. Although he makes use of his unconscious to solve a problem, he lacks confidence in this aspect of himself, he does not feel he can rely on it. He becomes alienated and despondent, questioning the point of what he is doing, recognizing that it has no meaning for him. The potential to feel alienated is signified by Uranus conjunct the Descendant, and the potential to lose hope is signified by Saturn semisextile Neptune. He has lost his way. He has let go of his particular vision or ambition.

The sense of loss and alienation, both from society and self, now pervades the rest of Michael's journey. The mole colony offers a delightful illustration of Saturn in Virgo, in that everyone is busy working and poring over maps and plans. But Michael is not a part of society. Nobody consults or informs him, he is ignored, and he places himself outside of society and feels estranged. Michael senses his failure and feels a huge sadness. It is the beginning of a realization of loss.

Michael is looking for peace. He wants to escape, to let his feelings evaporate. This is signified in his chart by the Mercury Neptune conjunction. In an attempt to get away from his painful feelings of alienation, he remembers an old addiction that once served as a defense against feeling.

The old mole has a wife and child and a cozy home: he is part of a family. Michael desperately wants to be loved and in a relationship with the old mole and his wife, who could be seen to represent the parents. Michael's longing to have a place within the family reflects his need to be unconditionally accepted and loved, as signified by Venus square Saturn. Venus rules the fourth house in Michael's chart, the house describing his early home life, and when square to Saturn, it can indicate that love had to be earned or was conditional. Deep feelings of rejection can arise from not having been accepted for oneself. Michael suggests to the old mole that he could live with them, but before the old mole responds, he sees that they have a child already, and assumes they will not want him, too. He shrugs it off. In part this describes how he anticipates rejection, and how he then dismisses his needs.

The old mole and his wife could be seen to represent internalized parental figures, aspects of himself Michael feels estranged from. Michael's alienation from the family connects significantly with his sense of alienation from society. Unable to find a place within the family, he later finds no place in society, and this brings grief. As yet, all this may be largely unconscious. Michael may need to recognize his losses and mourn them.

This process may help Michael find his place. Fulfillment often comes later in life for those with a strong Saturn, which is Michael's chart ruler.

OLIVIA'S SATURN JOURNEY

"I was a little brown mole, and when I rolled into a ball I felt really nice and good and safe. I watched myself from outside burrowing about. (Saturn square Uranus) For a moment, I looked like a hamster, stretched out, burrowing away, and trying to keep my head up and above it. (Saturn in the ninth, Sagittarius Ascendant)

"Then I decided to just get moving, and I felt much better. I had been a bit concerned because the earth was lovely and moist, but not hard, and I wondered if it would crumble. But then I realized that it was just right. It smelt very rich and was firm enough to stay intact, but was easy to burrow through. (Mars conjunct Saturn opposite Jupiter)

"So off I went. I moved, slanting downwards. Suddenly it all opened out, and I was in this large area. It felt like the room at the end of the tunnel. I had a light and was looking around. It felt good and I wanted to stay, but I knew I should be burrowing further. But it felt irrelevant because I felt I'd got to where I wanted to go. (Saturn in the ninth)

"I looked around and was thinking of starting another tunnel when I heard I'd encountered a boulder. Good, I thought, I'll go up and over the top, and I shot off, starting to burrow. (Jupiter opposite Saturn, Saturn square Uranus)

"As I burrowed, I was thinking that at least there had to be a top, and therefore an end, so I could get around. But then I thought that I could apply myself to the bottom and the sides. I thought about turning around but decided to continue. (Saturn in Libra in the ninth)

"Then I popped out of the ground and continued up to the top of the boulder. I had to go over, even though I wasn't burrowing. Afterwards, I thought it would have been easier to go around the sides.

"I sat at the top of the boulder wondering what to do next. Then I heard I was part of a colony. I was thrilled and went running back down to my original room. It was great to see everyone there. We were all chatting and socializing—all types, all ages. (Saturn in Libra)

"Our rules in the colony are:

    1) Not to hurt anyone. (Saturn conjunct Neptune)

    2) To do to others as you'd do to yourself. (Saturn in Libra)

"The mayor was in charge. He looked very stern and I felt very small by his left foot. I slept. (Moon conjunct Saturn)

"The wise person was a lady mole with pince-nez glasses and a lavender shawl. (Moon conjunct Saturn) I asked her what I should do about everything that was happening in my life.

"She said, 'Let go.' (Saturn square Uranus)

"I felt very panicky and shouted 'How? How? I can't!' I felt something sharp stick in my solar plexus. (Mars Saturn conjunction square Uranus)

"She was very calm and said, 'Just let go.' (Moon conjunct Saturn)

"I felt as though I was being carried off, and felt very dreamy and calm." (Moon Mars Saturn Neptune conjunction in Libra in the ninth)

Olivia illustrated some of the images from her journey and added this note: "Going over the top of the boulder seemed the only way, initially. However, looking at my picture, I noticed it was, in fact, the longest journey."

See page 34 for Olivia's chart. Olivia starts her journey with good feelings. She is happy with her lot. She has some momentary concerns, but then realizes that the soil is "just right." Things are just right in her world—the atmosphere, her environment, the conditions.

Olivia observes herself at work, indicating a sense of self-awareness and perspective, shown astrologically by Uranus. She is trying to keep her head above it. (classic Sagittarius Ascendant) She is not too embedded in the depths. Yet her tunnel slants downwards, and she is able to move down towards the unconscious. Later she has her own light, and she is able to create what she needs and what is helpful. She is resourceful and creative.

Olivia feels she should keep going though she has already arrived at where she wanted to go, perhaps reflecting that in her life Olivia keeps going though she is quite content with her life status.

When her ears tell her she has met a boulder, she tackles it with great enthusiasm. She is able to meet challenges and difficulties with optimism—a positive manifestation of Jupiter opposite Mars and Saturn. With a stellium in Libra, Olivia is able to think things through and resolve them satisfactorily. Her world doesn't collapse when she meets difficulties. She is not daunted and she keeps all her options open.

Olivia is thrilled to find she is part of a colony. The extremely sociable side of Libra is evident: She can mix with a wide range of people, and the whole atmosphere is social. The two rules of the colony are classic and basic to all religions, illustrating the reasonable and fair side of Libra as well as Oliva's innate sense of religion. (Saturn Neptune conjunction in Libra in the ninth house)

The mayor must be an inner father figure, and a rather stern one, again an expression of Saturn in the ninth house. Olivia feels safe with him. She sleeps, lapses into unconsciousness, signified by the Moon conjunct Saturn. She is very accepting, very trusting, and has no problem in accepting the mayor's authority. The flip side of accepting another's authority can be an abdication of your own authority. This doesn't seem to be the case here. Olivia simply feels secure with an internalized, rather strict father figure.

Olivia's wise person is a female mole, an embodiment of her Moon Saturn conjunction, and an inner mother figure. Her question is very broad and far-reaching, signified by the ninth house. Olivia is told to "let go," which panics her. Saturn signifies control, and the Saturn Uranus square signifies the potential to feel panic as well as the potential to let go. Her gut reaction is signified by the Moon and Mars, which Olivia has conjunct her Saturn, a planetary combination that indicates strong emotional reactions. She reacts to being out of control, yet when she does surrender to the wise mole's authority, her panic disappears and she feels safe and emotionally held. Olivia is able to accept her advice and is emotionally contained by her. She has an internalized mother figure that she can trust and rely upon. She ends her journey feeling calm, content, and in a dreamy state, a manifestation of her stellium in Libra in the ninth.

Olivia's footnote explains that although she felt impelled to go over the top of the boulder, this was not in fact the shortest route. Perhaps Olivia's normal reaction is to go "over the top," and only in retrospect does she see that it may not have been the best solution. A propensity to quick and excited reactions is signified by Jupiter, the planet of expansion, and by Uranus, the planet of unpredictability, both making aspects to her Libran planets.

All in all, this journey shows Olivia to be pretty happy with her lot. She has internalized Saturn's principle and incorporated it successfully into her psyche. Saturn is considered to be exalted in Libra, and Olivia illustrates Saturn's principle working at its best.

The two examples in this chapter represent two extremes. Most participants fall somewhere in between, having managed to incorporate Saturn's principle successfully into their life in some areas while still struggling in others. One participant asked her wise mole if she had to live underground with all the other moles. Her wise mole told her she had to be a part of society, not outside it. Another, with had Saturn on the IC, asked if she would find inner security. Another asked her wise mole if she would always be lonely. She has a Venus Saturn square. So while some participants are struggling to find their place within society, others have entirely different concerns, depending on Saturn's placement in their chart.

On the whole, those who have embodied Saturn's principle and worked within a career structure and taken on responsibilities in life have a far easier time on this journey. Those who have chosen to live outside mainstream society may or may not have a difficult time, depending on how much responsibility their lifestyle entails and what their intrinsic attitude to Saturn's principle is. Whatever our issue, what is clear is that if we can internalize Saturn's principle, we can be far happier within ourselves.

CHAPTER 9

Uranus

⛢

Uranus is the first of the three transpersonal planets, which means its domain, along with Neptune and Pluto's, is beyond the personal. Uranus is considered the higher octave of Mercury, and while Mercury rules thought and communication, Uranus is connected to universal thought and communication. Uranus rules such things as satellite transmissions, radio waves, computers, and all the new-fangled gadgetry of our technological age. Those who are particularly gifted in these fields are likely to have Uranus strongly featured in their chart. (Strength is judged by a close conjunction or hard aspect to a personal planet or the Ascendant or MC.)

All states of alienation are Uranus' domain. This covers the gamut, from those who are exiles to those who stand out as different or eccentric, from those who feel cut off, frozen, numb, disconnected, or disassociated from themselves to those with states of mental disintegration and fragmentation. Those who have taken LSD have had a Uranian experience, in which perception becomes fragmented and distorted. The popular idiom of the counterculture of the sixties and seventies was that acid "blew your mind." Afterwards, life never looked the same again. Perhaps they thought they had glimpsed enlightenment. Regardless, they had certainly been in touch with Uranus' principle.

All shocks and surprises are Uranus' domain, and we are most susceptible to these when we have a Uranus transit. Uranus is associated with waking up to a lightning realization that can be both shocking and liberating.
Those of us with Uranus strongly featured in our chart will have a capacity
to shock others. Madonna is an example with her Sun conjunct Uranus.
Anyone who chooses not to fit in, who stands outside mainstream society
for whatever reason, is likely to have a prominent Uranus.

Uranus is associated with freedom: the freedom to be different, the freedom to be our own unique self. With Uranus emphasized, we may well have
unconventional attitudes to life. We are not afraid to stand by our beliefs
and do not mind what the consensus opinion is. Those with a strong
Uranus are often ahead of their time, and the rest of society eventually
catches up with them. For instance, 25 years ago it was considered cranky
and eccentric to be vegetarian, whereas now it is considered healthy and is
commonplace. Most restaurants cater to vegetarians these days. Public
opinion has shifted. Although it was once Uranian to be a vegetarian, now
that it's become mainstream, it is no longer.

Rebellion is a key Uranian characteristic. Those of us with a strong
Uranus will rebel against different things at different stages in our life.
Particularly when young, those with a strong Uranus can be downright con-
trary. It's as if contradicting others is an automatic response: rebellion just
for the sake of it. As we mature, we can channel our rebellious streak into
worthwhile causes, and some of us become political activists.

Uranus is extreme. Those with a prominent Uranus who do enter the
political arena can veer either to the extreme left or the extreme right. What
distinguishes the Uranian politician is his or her lack of moderation. Even
those not actively involved with any mainstream politics will still have
strong political ideals. They will be drawn to any movement concerned with
liberation, from animal rights, to abortion rights, to human rights. Given
certain circumstances, someone with a strong Uranus can become a fanat-
ic. The so-called "lunatic fringe" is Uranian.

Uranus' principle is objective. It is concerned with the truth of a matter. Those of us who have a strong Uranus can offer perspective on situations. We look at ourselves and others with detachment. We view things from an impersonal vantage point. This emphasis on perspective, objectivity, and detachment can come across as rather cold and insensitive to others' feelings. Uranus is concerned with honesty. This is its god. Whereas Neptune knows all truth is relative, Uranus believes there is an absolute truth.

Uranus takes commitment very seriously. Commitment is total and absolute, so making a commitment can become very threatening. Typically, those of us with a strong Uranus struggle when it comes to making a commitment, even when for all intents and purposes committing does not much change the situation. We might refuse to marry, seeing marriage as a noose around our neck, when we have been living together as man and wife anyway. This could also relate to our principles, as we may not believe in marriage and want a more open relationship. Some with a strong Uranus adopt alternative lifestyles, such as gay or lesbian.

The guided imagery that follows presents various symbolic scenarios that put us in touch with Uranus' principle, so that we may see how this principle operates within us. The journey was written for use by a group. If you are doing the journey alone, use the adapted version marked "For Individuals." Before you begin this journey, please refer to *Some Guidelines Before Going on a Guided Imagery Journey* in Chapter 1 and go through the *Relaxation Exercise* given there.

Guided Imagery Journey on Uranus' Principle

— I want you to imagine there is no ceiling above you and that you can gaze right up into the night sky. (short pause)

— You can see the stars, the big stars and then the farthest away stars, the tiny specks of light. (pause)

— I want you to imagine yourself rising up, up into the night sky. (short pause)

— **For groups:** Imagine yourself just a little way up, and now look down and see us all together in this room below. (short pause)

— As you look down on our group, let yourself know what you think of it. (short pause)

— **For individuals:** Imagine yourself just a little way up, and now look down and see yourself in the room below. (short pause)

— As you look down, let yourself know what you think of yourself. (short pause)

— How does it look to you from up here? (pause)

— Now go up even further into the night sky until this room is no longer distinguishable. Look down and see the shape of your country with the surrounding sea. (pause)

— What do you think of your country and the way of life of your countrymen? (long pause)

— Now rise up even further. (short pause)

— You are free of the Earth's gravity. (short pause)

— You are so far up that your country is not distinguishable. The earth is just a large, round ball below. (short pause)

— Look down at life on Earth and let yourself know what you think of it. (pause)

— Focus on some of the popular ideas of our time and see how you fit in with them. What is your relationship to them? (pause)

— Now rise up even further. (short pause)

— Enjoy the feeling of being free in space. (short pause)

— The Earth is now just a dot, and you're up among the stars. (short pause)

— Some stars are huge and brilliant, some white, some blue—all colors. (short pause)

— This world is extraordinary. (short pause)

— Around you are tremendous electric storms and energy turbulence. Blue lightning zigzags through space like flashing neon lights. Stars explode and disappear. (short pause)

— It's like an amazing fireworks display, magical and awe inspiring. You watch in wonder. (pause)

— And now, start to come back down. (short pause)

— The Earth is getting closer. (short pause)

— Now your country is visible. (short pause)

— And now this room is visible. (short pause)

— And you are back in the room. (short pause)

— As you lie or sit here, I want you to remember what you saw up there in the sky. And I want you to imagine: If the electric storm had a voice, what would it have been saying to you? (short pause)

— What was its message to you? (long pause)

— Now, think if there's something you're scared of doing. (short pause)

— It's something that would make you feel more alive. (pause)

— Is there something you'd like to change in your life? (pause)

— Is there something or someone you're scared of letting go of? (pause)

— Think of ways you could be more yourself, more your own unique person. (pause)

When you are ready, open your eyes and come back into the room.

Some Guidelines for How to Interpret Your Journey

In this guided imagery journey we are given an opportunity to gain perspective on our lives, to get in touch with what we really think about ourselves, our country, our world, and the universe in a detached way. To facilitate this, we imagine ourselves literally detached from the earth's confines. We come at this in four stages. In the first stage we detach ourselves from our immediate surroundings. We rise up from the room we are in, from ourselves, and from the group we are with (where applicable), and we allow ourselves to know what we think about ourselves and the group. Some people become self-conscious at this stage and can't go further. But most can ascend to get a bird's-eye view of the situation below. At this stage there is the opportunity to consider our personal identity.

In the second stage, we rise up higher into the sky and have a wider perspective. We can see our country down below, which acts as a metaphor for broader questions and issues. We move on from our personal identity to consider our national identity.

Some will identify with the characteristics of their country while others will feel more separate, or even alienated. Some may identify with a stratum of society or a race. Others identify more broadly, with something beyond their country, and that might leave them feeling alienated from a sense of national identity.

During the third stage of the guided imagery journey, we imagine ourselves outside the Earth's gravitational pull, clear of its influence. Here we can begin to think about questions and issues from a place of even greater detachment. We look at forces that affect our world, at global issues and our individual opinions regarding them. We have risen stage by stage toward loftier issues, more abstract thoughts, into the realm of impersonal ideas. Those with a strong Uranus in their chart tend to feel at home in this exciting arena, enjoying the mental stimulation.

In the final stage of the Uranus journey we travel to the outer reaches of our galaxy. Earth becomes a small dot in space. We are totally liberated from the usual confines of Earth life and able to witness the energy of a higher dimension. This place offers us maximum perspective on the universe. We behold the extraordinary world of deep space with all its energy and tumult. As we watch the scene unfold, we are filled by the experience, and identify on some level with what we witness. Once back on firm ground, we can begin to find meaning in our experience and express it in language. We have had a Uranian experience par excellence. Some people find this stage of the journey frightening, far beyond what is familiar and safe, but, in the main, participants feel uplifted and liberated.

Once back in the room, participants are asked to ground their experience, to articulate the message of their experience and its potential impact on their lives. Participants are given the opportunity to reflect on various aspects of their lives and consider, in the light of their experience, any changes they might want to make. This further grounds their experience.

Check that you are firmly back on earth and in the room when this journey is complete. If not feeling properly grounded, do a grounding exercise.

The exercise which follows can be used whenever you feel ungrounded, for whatever reason. Barefooted, stand with feet apart and arms slightly raised and stretched out to your sides. Feel invisible threads running from the center of your being down through your legs and the soles of your feet, into the ground below. This is your imaginary root. At the same time, feel an invisible thread running upwards through the top of your head into the sky. Be simultaneously aware of your connection to the sky above and to the earth below. Stretch, feel your feet on the ground, and keep your focus on being rooted to the earth.

Other People's Journeys

Let us go on to look at the charts and journeys of two women who did this journey with me on July 31, 1993. The accounts are reproduced here verbatim, as they recorded them at the time. Where I have made connections back to their natal chart I have inserted the astrological signifiers in parentheses in their text.

ELISE'S URANUS JOURNEY

"First of all I was in Greece in a Taverna with an open roof. It was at night and the sky was full of stars. It was a beautiful setting. (Moon in Sagittarius)

"Then I was floating above the room and looking down on us all. My first reaction, I'm afraid, was to start to laugh and think, 'What are we doing?!' I thought it was hilarious. Then I stopped laughing and felt very bad about this. (Mercury sesquiquadrate Uranus)

"I became a silvery-white tornado and also a silver line shooting backward and forward. Then I created a storm in the room and papers were blowing about, and there was total chaos, and I was also causing it to rain. (Sun trine Uranus, Mercury sesquiquadrate Uranus)

"Then I was out in space looking down on Great Britain. I was still the silver tornado. My thoughts about Great Britain were: Everyone is too prim and proper. (Jupiter and Saturn in Capricorn) People are not friendly enough, and there is not much community spirit. Also, there is not enough value on children and the role of mothers. I wondered if in the war days people were more for each other and they all knew each other down the street. I felt that perhaps African countries may know more about being part of each other and enjoying being a community. (Uranus conjunct the Ascendant in Leo, Moon trine Uranus)

"Then I was farther out in space and looking down on the whole world. My thoughts were: All the countries are too broken up. There is too much racism. This is frightening. We are living with the time bomb of racism ticking away! (Mars opposite Pluto) We should grow and be conscious that we are all part of the same, and do good for the whole World Family! We should get away from all this materialism, which seems to be the value for everything and all government actions. This is getting us nowhere and only in a worse mess. We should all become more spiritual in our attitudes. (Uranus conjunct the Ascendant, Sun Jupiter Pluto grand trine)

"Further up, the world is just a speck. This is brilliant! I feel as if I am a big, yellow sun, and I can feel the magnificent warmth and glow all through me. There are lots of different-colored suns all around me, some blue, some red. Then I am the silver tornado and also the silvery streak which darts back and forth in a straightish line. I am looking in wonder at all of space around me. It seems as if all is moving about to a wonderful orchestra of music. I have picked up the electrical atmosphere and become full of sparks. (Sun trine Uranus)

"I really want to stay here but I am being told to go down. I feel like a firecracker, and the tornado is very crackly/sparkly. (Sun conjunct the MC trine Uranus conjunct the Ascendant)

"My feelings about this time have to do with greater freedom in relationships now. It is good that people can choose to marry or to live together. Women are more independent and can do anything, really, and have equality. (Moon trine Uranus)

"I am floating down under a big parachute. When I get nearer to the ground, I can see the color of the parachute is actually black and it must engulf me and put out all my sparks. 'I can't let people see me like this!' (Sun trine Uranus, Sun trine Pluto, Sun square Saturn)

"Q. What do you really want to change about your life to make it more exciting? Relationship? Quickly, No! Job? Yes, to find a suitable career eventually, when the time is right. It is good to feel part of a group of people and not to work on my own. This gives me a sense of identity through what I do and greater security through work and being part of an organization or team. (Uranus conjunct Ascendant in Leo)

"Relationship? Sometimes it may seem tempting to change and be free, but I know I can't. I need limitations, a base. I have a good situation to develop and be myself. J. and I are good for each other, and there are no rules and regulations, within reason, of course. But I must be tied down, and I appreciate J.'s and my relationship. (Sun trine Uranus, Sun square Saturn)

"Second question (can't remember exactly what was asked)
Answer: We are all part of each other and everything is a part of me." (Mercury in Pisces sesquiquadrate Uranus)

See page 29 for Elise's chart. Elise enjoyed this journey and felt very much in her element. With Uranus in the first conjunct her Ascendant, we would expect her to feel identified with Uranus' principle. She begins the journey mocking the seriousness of the situation. These feelings are quickly followed by guilt. Perhaps Elise becomes self-conscious as she begins to separate from the group and gain perspective, which leads to momentarily feeling alienated.

Elise becomes a silvery-white tornado, which gives her far more power and control as she moves through space. There is obvious phallic symbolism here; perhaps having felt estranged, Elise connects to a masterful side of herself. The need to take control of herself and situations, and the ease with which Elise does so, is reflected in the grand trine in her chart involving the Sun, Jupiter, and Pluto. This shows a potential to be extremely effective.

She then creates a storm in the room, which implies an internal storm. Elise places the storm *in* the room, so perhaps it is connected to her feelings about the group. Papers are blowing about, which could represent a flurry of ideas, and there is total chaos, perhaps an externalization of Elise's internal chaos. Certainly Uranus rising has the potential to be extremely disruptive, and perhaps Elise touches briefly on this capacity within herself at the start of this journey. It begins to rain, reflecting a change to sadder feelings.

She reflects that Great Britain is too prim and proper. Both horoscopes most commonly used for Great Britain—the 1066 and the 1701 charts—have the Sun in Capricorn. Britain is a country known for its stiff-upper-lip mentality and class system. Elise has Saturn in Capricorn, square to her Aries Sun and quincunx Uranus, so perhaps she tunes into the way the culture is prim and proper because it echoes the internal conflict between her conventional, conservative side and her more independent, freedom-loving side.

Elise's thoughts are of her immediate environment and her place within it. She rues the loss of community spirit and harks back to a time when crisis threw people together. She speculates that African countries know more about being a community. With her Moon in Sagittarius, Elise has a strong affinity to foreign places. Uranus trines both the Sun and Moon and conjuncts the Ascendant, so Elise is likely to identify with her ideals and beliefs, to feel them as part of herself.

As Elise moves further out in space, she is concerned by the fragmentation of the world. This may reflect her own internal fragmentation. However, there is plenty of division in the real world to warrant concern, and with such a strong Uranus, Elise is likely to have a political bent. Likewise is her concern with racism. This could be seen to reflect an inner conflict between her "dark" and "light" sides. Elise may be concerned by her own darkness, which is scary and threatening to her, and the "World

Family" she speaks of could reflect her own need to integrate these two sides of herself. We can see this possibility astrologically: The brightness of Uranus rising in Leo, the Sun in Aries on the MC, and Moon in Sagittarius are the parts of Elise's chart she most identifies with. She is less likely to identify with the Mars Pluto opposition and Saturn in Capricorn, which are far "darker" energies. This is not to diminish the very real problems of racism within the world or the need for the values Elise speaks of, but it is important to show the roots of Elise's idealism within her psyche.

In the next phase of the guided imagery journey, Elise thoroughly enjoys herself. Despite having no air in her chart, she is in her element up here. Elise picks up the electrical atmosphere and becomes full of sparks. She feels like a firecracker, and the tornado is "crackly/sparkly!" This is signified by Uranus rising along with the fiery emphasis in her chart.

Elise's thoughts turn to women's position in relationships and society, which reflect her own need for independence. As she lands, she imagines she is floating down under a black parachute, and that it is going to engulf her and put out all her sparks. Black we associate with Saturn and Pluto. This has to be signified by the square from Saturn and the trine from Pluto to her Sun; these darker principles can engulf her sparkly energy and extinguish it.

When thinking about what she wants to change in her life, Elise first considers, then quickly moves away from her relationship, as if even thinking about making any changes is threatening. Further on, she acknowledges her desire for freedom, but independence threatens the side of her that wants stability and security. She appraises her needs in a rational and realistic way.

Elise considers what she wants from her career. She prefers to be part of a group rather than to work alone (signified by Uranus rising and Aquarius on the Descendant). This enhances her sense of identity (signified by the Sun on the MC), and she gains greater security through being part of an organization (signified by the square to Saturn in Capricorn). Elise elegantly illustrates the symbolism of her chart.

Elise ends her journey with the Neptunian statement "We are all part of each other, and everything is a part of me," signified by her Mercury in Pisces sesquiquadrate Uranus. Here we have the idealism of Neptune and Uranus coming together, which Elise embodies in her spiritual quest, as illustrated more vividly in some of her other journeys.

OLIVIA'S URANUS JOURNEY

"I was lying in Nuyeba by the Red Sea, with M., a partner of long standing, and E., who is my current partner, looking at the shooting stars in the night sky and listening to the sea. When I had to go up, I wanted them to come with me. (Uranus in Cancer in the seventh house)

"I was floating upwards and everything felt very ethereal. Then I was looking down on the group. We were in a circle which was very contained. We had electric colors (auras) around us: Daniel—turquoise, Babs—yellow, Ann—green, Elise—orange, and I had cerise and silver.

"Then I went higher. I was swimming upwards, doing the breast stroke. I stopped and looked at Great Britain. The colors were royal blue and black. I thought, 'It's cold and hard—black and white—isolated.' (Mars Saturn conjunction square Uranus)

"Then I was away from the earth's surface. The air was so fresh and clean. I looked down on the earth, and it was covered by a massive magnetic force, and the energy was beginning to go inward. It was oppressive and suffocating. I sliced it in four like an apple, and the poisons and toxins began to escape. The cuts were very clean. I knew it was ruthless, but it was the only way. (Mars square Uranus)

"The ideas of the world—the new age time. 'This is my time. I have waited a long time, but now it's time for me to do what I want and develop creativity.' (Sun conjunct the Ascendant, Uranus focal planet in T-square)

"I went higher. The colors were amazing, and I was whizzing around. I became two people linked together—Aryan types, a tall, blond, handsome man and a tall, blonde, beautiful woman—both dressed in silver jump-suits. But they were both too beautiful, too perfect. (Uranus in the seventh)

"I wanted the electric storm to be silver, not blue, to match the silver crescent moon. I came down quickly. It felt hard, like I was imploding.

"The electric storm would have said 'throw me a line'—a way of getting from where I am to where I want to be—using my creativity. What can I change about myself? 'I don't want to be a nurse,' and I stamp on the bedpan and throw it away. I want help and support. I want to create something new." (Sun square Moon, Uranus in the seventh)

See page 34 for Olivia's chart. Olivia starts her journey by the Red Sea. She chooses a hot, foreign place, as reflects the emphasis in Sagittarius and the ninth house in her chart. The Red Sea may also have other symbolic significance; it was the parting of the Red Sea that helped the Israelites find the promised land. This myth may have personal meaning for Olivia.

Olivia wanted to travel upwards with both her current partner and her ex-partner. Perhaps she would like to be with both of her lovers and have a more unconventional lifestyle, something Uranus in the seventh house would signify.

As she floats upwards she is in touch with Neptune on the MC, insofar as she feels ethereal and can see the auras of those in the group. Her view of the group is that it is contained, which may indicate that Olivia finds the group safe and feels contained by it.

Olivia saw Great Britain as "cold and hard—black and white—isolated." Great Britain is an island, literally isolated, surrounded by sea, apart from other countries. Perhaps this isolation reflects Olivia's own feelings of isolation. The cold and hard, black and white that Olivia perceives is perhaps reflected in her chart by the Mars Saturn conjunction squared to Uranus. These are not qualities that Olivia exhibits, but they do fit these signifiers.

During the next stage Olivia is in touch with an oppressive and suffocating energy that is toxic, as well as with a ruthless part of herself that is capable of doing what is necessary. Her capacity to act in a decisive way, along with a low tolerance for oppressive or suffocating circumstances, are all signified by the Mars Uranus square in her chart. Poisons and toxins are signified by Neptune, which is on the MC in Olivia's chart and conjuncts her Mars. Planets found on the MC are often projected out onto the world, the world becoming an extension of our experience of mother. What we find here is an urge for the clean-cut clarity of Mars Uranus in the face of the toxic, suffocating, magnetic energy of Mars Neptune. Olivia literally cuts the world into quarters in her imagery, which metaphorically reflects her capacity to cut through any nonsense and to react forcefully.

In the final stage, Olivia glimpses the perfect union, but realizes it is too perfect—it lacks reality. She mentions Aryan types, with connotations of the fascist ideal, which Uranus could signify. With Uranus in the house of partnerships, Olivia has an idealized concept of relationships. This idealization could be in response to the pain she is likely to have encountered in her life through her relationships.

Olivia has a stellium in Libra, the sign associated with partnerships, indicating that her relationship needs are complex. She has Neptune conjunct her Libra MC, indicating that she has tremendous romantic and idealistic yearnings around love. She has a Venus Pluto square, adding depth and further complexity to her relationship needs. To cap it all, she has Uranus, the planet associated with extremes, freedom, and independence in the house of partnerships. Perhaps Olivia yearns for the fusion of the couple in her fantasy, for perfection, yet she knows this is unrealistic.

Olivia wants support for her creativity. She speaks of having waited, but that it is now her time. She wants to be thrown a line. She no longer wants to be a nurse. Nurse equals care-giver, but Olivia now wants some care and support for herself. She wants to be free of the onerous and perhaps demeaning, imprisoning task of caregiving. She demonstrates this by stamping on the bedpan, to free herself to explore her own creativity.

We see here a need for the Moon's principle, the nurturer, to support the Sun's principle, the creative heart of the chart. In Olivia's chart, Moon and Sun are in square. These two principles battle it out for space in her life. She spends too much time caring for others rather than nurturing herself and her own creative spirit. She knows what she wants from others and feels it is their lack of support that traps her (signified by Uranus in the seventh), but she also needs to find a way of better taking care of herself.

Unlike some of the other planetary principle journeys, there is little overt emotional content in this one's. To be in the far-flung reaches of space is, symbolically, to be in the realm of intellectual ideas. This is Uranus' realm: detached, abstract thought. The Uranus journey appeals to the participants' senses of idealism. I have analyzed their idealism from psychological and astrological points of view, integrating it with their psyche. I have tried to demonstrate that our ideas are as much a part of ourselves as our feelings.

Both Elise and Olivia thoroughly enjoyed this journey. Those who are less able to respond usually have an emphasis of earth and water in their charts, or a strong Saturn or Pluto, and probably are at greater ease with the guided imagery journeys which draw on the feeling realm. Nevertheless, it can be very helpful to those who identify more with their feeling sides to examine what they *think* about things, too. Most participants are left feeling uplifted and inspired by this journey.

CHAPTER 10

Neptune

Ψ

Neptune is the second of the transpersonal planets, symbolizing our search for oneness with God or a higher spiritual being, and for a higher level of consciousness. On a more everyday level, this reflects a longing for the ideal, for perfection, which leaves those with Neptune featured strongly in their charts (in a hard aspect to a personal planet, the Ascendant, or the MC) susceptible to feelings of disappointment and disillusionment when life fails to live up to their dreams.

Neptune is associated with aspirations of the highest order. It symbolizes our yearning for oneness with the divine, and those of us with Neptune emphasized in our chart are very in tune with the oneness of life, capable of experiencing a oneness with nature and with fellow human beings. The downside to this is a lack of a sense of a separate self. We tend to merge with anything and everything. We have a chameleonlike quality and can lack discrimination. Our psyche can be spongelike, soaking up and merging with whatever is in the emotional atmosphere. This gives us a tremendous advantage in situations which require empathy, but we have great difficulty in protecting ourselves, as this facility is not something that can be easily switched on and off. We are susceptible to feeling contaminated and poisoned by certain atmospheres. We pick up on the feelings of others whether we want to or not, and do not have a clear sense of ourselves as separate.

It could be argued we are not separate from one another anyway, that the whole idea of individuality is an egocentric myth, that we really are all one. Those of us who are strongly Neptunian do not have a clear sense of where we end and another begins, very like the relationship of a newborn baby to its mother. Most of us experience some degree of these feelings in our close relationships. Everybody can experience feelings of both love and hate towards the same person or thing. In a relationship, one person, inspired by idealism, may express only their love feelings and deny the hate. The other partner may then identify with and express all the negative feelings for both partners. This happens with feelings like closeness and distance, need and denial of need, and so on. The various feelings inherent in the relationship will, at different times, be embodied by one partner, while the other partner denies them altogether. The couple polarize and become more extreme in their positions. The feelings will run between two people a bit like the sand in an egg timer. Those of us with a strong Neptune are particularly tuned into this phenomenon in all areas of life. We can never be certain who we are or what we think or believe. Life is never simple for us, as we are always influenced by the thoughts and feelings of those around us.

Those of us with a strong Neptune are always kindly and sensitive to the feelings of others. We identify with what we imagine them to feel and will relate to them from this standpoint. This can lead to others perceiving us as dishonest, changing our colors to suit the situation. Our honesty and integrity are always relative to our surroundings, and we are never separate from what surrounds us. We do not possess the absoluteness of those with Uranus emphasized.

Consistency is not our strong point. Indeed, we may perceive consistency as rigidity because we so value adaptability and sacrifice. We can be seen as deceitful and treacherous, but this is because we are being judged from a standpoint that is alien to us.

Those of us with a strong Neptune often have the sense that anything is possible, that the sky is the limit. This can make it difficult for us to settle on one direction, one track in life. We can be overwhelmed by the infinite possibilities we feel are open to us. Others may see us as chasing rainbows, and while some of us may achieve what was seemingly impossible, some of us can end up with very little to show for all our efforts. This doesn't concern us, however, as it is following our dream that counts. Concrete achievement is not crucial to us. That is Saturn's domain.

Those with a strong Neptune can appear "spaced out," confused, all over the place, not grounded in everyday reality. Often, Neptunian types are habitually late, as they have a poor sense of time. They can live in a fantasy world, or can make a rapid retreat into their fantasies whenever ordinary reality becomes uncongenial.

Some of us may, at times, lose our connection with everyday reality completely. The world of our imagination takes precedence, providing an escape from feelings that are too painful for us to process. We may even become psychotic. Some of us will dip in and out of mild psychosis, seeing what seems to a more rational person to be fantastical connections and meanings in everyday events. Our imagination becomes distorted as we attempt to cope with boredom, drabness, or feelings of pain. Our world will settle into a more normal state as our painful feelings subside.

Neptune is associated with alcohol and drug abuse. Those with a strong Neptune are searching for an elusive something beyond the mundane, something spiritual which they may think they will find in a bottle of spirits or a drug induced high. It is fitting that Alcoholics Anonymous and Narcotics Anonymous base their programs of recovery on an appreciation of the spiritual realm, as this is precisely what so many addicts are searching for. Alcohol and drug addiction are usually a form of escape from the pain of quotidian reality, and those of us with a strong Neptune have both addictive and escapist tendencies. For many of us, this may simply take the form of going to the cinema or watching too much television.

Neptune is the higher octave of Venus, and whereas Venus rules personal love, Neptune is concerned with universal love. Neptunian love and compassion is nonspecific. It's love on a grand scale. On television, Michael

Jackson says, "I love you all," pledging his love indiscriminately to all who are viewing, to people he has never met. This is Neptunian love. His fans may reciprocate, but it is a fantasy, an ideal they have built up around him that they love, so it is still a Neptunian kind of love.

As Uranus is associated with the collective ideas of our time, so Neptune is associated with collective feelings, feelings that sway the masses, and these are particularly expressed through fashion, pop music, the cinema, drama, and the arts. Neptune is associated with fame, glamour, and the film world. Those with a strong Neptune can feel at home in a world of make-believe. The singer Deborah Harry once said she wrote the songs that were already in everyone's mind. So as soon as her song was heard it was recognized. People felt they knew it. This recognition of something moving within the collective unconscious is Neptunian, and those of us with a strong Neptune have a capacity to express it for our time. Fashion designers tune in to what is going to be in vogue next for the man and woman on the street, then anyone with a strong Neptune picks up this sudden irresistible urge to wear citrus shades, flared trousers, satin, or whatever. People think they are simply following fashion, but actually they are often simultaneously tuning in to the collective unconscious. Films that capture the spirit of the times are similarly conceived by those "plugged in" to this Neptunian realm.

Neptune moves slowly, remaining in each sign for about fourteen years, and each sign colors the theme of idealization emerging in the collective. For instance, those born with Neptune in Libra grew up as the "flower generation," the "hippies" of the sixties and seventies, full of idealized notions around relationships. The popular philosophy around relationships changed completely, and one result was a growing divorce rate.

The personal planets in hard aspect to Neptune in our chart will show which drives within us become idealized, unrealistic, and refined. The house in which Neptune falls will indicate an area of life likely to be deified, in which we are our most idealistic and prone to illusion. For instance, those of us with Neptune in the fourth may need our home to be ideal and perfect in some way. It may be a place of retreat, a haven of peace and quiet, like a temple. At the same time, we may idealize one of our parents, usually the father, around whom, for one reason or another, there may be a lack of reality. The less reality there is to make an impact, the more we can invent what we want to believe. This can lead to painful feelings of disappointment when the fantasy dissolves.

In the guided imagery that follows, various symbolic scenarios are presented that will put us in touch with Neptune's principle, so that we may experience how this principle operates within us. Before you begin this journey, please refer to *Some Guidelines Before Going on a Guided Imagery Journey* in Chapter 1 and go through the *Relaxation Exercise* given there.

Guided Imagery Journey on Neptune's Principle

— Imagine you are in a meadow by a lily pond. (short pause)

— The day is warm and lazy and you feel relaxed and happy. (short pause)

— You bask in the warmth of the sun, aware of the scents and sounds around you. (pause)

— You pass through a transparent film and enter the magical world of fairyland. (short pause)

— Here you can be invisible, change shape at whim, and totally disappear and reappear somewhere else. (pause)

— You can float on the lilies, nestle in flowers, fly, talk to the butterflies, dragonflies, and birds, play on the flower stems, and drink nectar. (long pause)

— Your world is full of song and music. (pause)

— Anything is possible. (pause)

— All your dreams can come true. (pause)

— Allow yourself to imagine what they would be. (pause)

— Create your own ideal, perfect world. It doesn't have to be fairyland, but it can be the seemingly impossible. It's your vision of perfection. (long pause)

— Are there any dangers in your world? (pause)

— What do you do in your world? (short pause)

— How do you all relate? (pause)

— Do you paint, sing, make music, meditate, or pray together? (pause)

— You can make a wish here. (short pause)

— Let yourself know what you most yearn for. (pause)

— Now ask for it. (short pause)

— And know it will be granted. (short pause)

— It's now time to return, so prepare to leave behind this world you've created. (short pause)

— Pass back through fairyland, and back through the transparent film into the meadow by the lily pond. (short pause)

When you are ready, open your eyes and come back into the room.

Some Guidelines for How to Interpret Your Journey

The journey starts by creating a scenario that induces feelings of ease and well-being in participants. Everyone enjoys the first part of this journey, responding to the idealized atmosphere they've conjured up. It is setting the tone for what is to come, as participants are led further and further from everyday reality.

Participants then pass through a transparent film, evocative of *Alice In Wonderland* or the Narnia fairy tales, and find themselves transported to the magical world of a fairyland where anything is possible. They are in a world of make-believe where everything is idyllic. Most participants revel and take delight in this imagery, embellishing it with their own fantasies of fairyland. A suspension of disbelief has been achieved.

From this point on, participants are free to imagine their own ideal world. Here they can get in touch with what perfection is for them, unhindered by the constraints of what is ordinarily possible. Some participants remain in fairyland, but many go on to create their own ideal world. We also see what concerns participants about the world they live in.

Participants are asked if there are any dangers in their ideal world. Many do not see any, but if they do, these dangers are always relevant and need to be explored afterward. One woman with Neptune in Scorpio inconjunct Venus fantasized that the boundaries between people broke down so that there was a great feeling of community. Her fear, which accompanied this ideal scenario, was that it would lead to "free love," which gave her concern for her marriage.

Participants are given time to explore their ideal world, which allows them to focus on some of the details of how this world is constructed, and how people relate to one another. What participants create is always something to talk through afterwards

Participants are asked if they paint, sing, make music, meditate, or pray together, all Neptunian pursuits. Being asked in this way is tantamount to suggesting to participants that, in fact, they do some of these activities. They are then free to imagine which activities they practice. Most participants will select the activities that most appeal to them and go on to imagine the contexts in which they occur. This autosuggestion adds a further Neptunian dimension to the imagery journey, and gives participants a chance to be in touch with something they may subsequently like to incorporate into their lives.

Finally, participants are invited to make a wish to acknowledge something they long for. Some participants are surprised by what they wish for, discovering an important, previously unacknowledged longing, while others reconnect with a familiar longing. Recognizing a longing is the first step towards making it a reality. There is a saying, be careful what you wish for—it may come true.

As with all journeys, it is important that participants return from the world they have created, back to the world they left behind.

Other People's Journeys

Let's look at the charts and journeys of a man and a woman who have been on this journey with me. Ann and Joe took this journey on September 11, 1993, and April 29, 1996, respectively. The accounts are reproduced here verbatim, as they were recorded at the time. Where I have made connections back to their natal chart, I have inserted the astrological signifiers in parentheses.

ANN'S NEPTUNE JOURNEY

"The field was full of long grass and white wildflowers. I was a girl with long blonde hair. (Venus sextile Neptune) The lily pond had large pads and white flowers, rather choked and overgrown a bit with weeds, no clearly defined shape. It was lovely and warm and relaxed in the grass. White butterflies flew around. Went to fairyland, colors changed to purple, pinks, blues…fairies flew about, elves and pixies, too. I was taken back to my grandmother's garden as a child. I saw myself as I was then, in the garden 'talking to the fairies.' Then I became a fairy and flew into a dandelion. Unpleasant nectar. Flew to lily pad—much nicer—rather sweet, settled there. Mozart's music playing all around, perfect through flowers, color, perfume, trees. (Mercury conjunct Neptune in the third house) My home was comfortable, near water. Food and drink always available, enough for everyone. People got on well, in harmony, no arguments or quarrels, everyone respects everyone's privacy. (Mercury Neptune conjunction in Libra in the third, Sun in Scorpio on the IC) I am in a home with someone who supports and cares for me as I am, though I never see this person, but just know they are there. I have the ability to fly—we all do in this world and can visit wherever we like and are always welcome. (Venus square Saturn) My talent and love is to dance, Spanish, fiery dancing that people come to see me perform. I love the music, rhythm, costume, and pride of it. (Leo Ascendant, Venus in Sagittarius in the fifth) Sometimes I do ballet. As a group, we often dance to the beat of a drum in a circle in harmony together. At night we commune with the stars and feel at one with the world and each other. There are artists of all kinds in this world. My wish is to be happy and content in life and have no regrets. However, I am aware of underlying danger. (Pluto rising, Mars in the first)

"I return via fairyland. I again see the child—me—asking 'why?' A very moving and upsetting moment. I see my face as a child looking so questioningly at me, and I don't know the answer. The look hurts me deeply. I then go back through the barrier to the safety of the field where I feel warm, but I can't forget the look of my childhood, reproaching me." (Moon biquintile Saturn, Moon trine Neptune, Mercury Neptune conjunction)

See page 28 for Ann's chart. Ann starts her journey as a girl with long, blonde hair, though she does not in reality have long, blonde hair. On these journeys Ann has always changed her appearance to suit the planetary principle. Her facility for this is shown by Pluto, the planet of transformation, conjunct her Ascendant, her outer appearance. One imagines this facility is something she employs in her life on a subtler level.

Ann's imagery is full of the innocence of childhood. There are white flowers in the field, white lilies on the lily pond, and the butterflies are white. White is a color we associate with purity and virginity; she has returned to her childhood. Later, Ann is back in her grandmother's garden as a child, remembering how she used to talk to the fairies. This memory, not in itself painful, triggered some extremely painful realizations. Ann connected emotionally to her "inner child" and began to see things through her eyes. Through this connection, something new for her, she began to realize how hurt she had been as a child. We glimpse this pain on her Moon guided imagery journey, but there it was only recognized on an intellectual level. We spoke then of the fact that she had abandoned aspects of herself, aspects she had disassociated from because they were painful.

Ann ends this journey seeing her abandoned inner child reproaching her. She was deeply upset by this journey. It was the most painful of all the journeys for Ann, the one that precipitated her decision to go into counseling for a time.

Early in the guided imagery journey, Ann describes the lily pond as rather choked and overgrown with weeds, with no clearly defined shape. We glimpse here the tangle of ill-defined feelings she subsequently connects to, lying beneath the rather idyllic surface.

Ann's home is comfortable. It is near water, there is food and drink always available—basic survival needs are met—and there is privacy, all signified by the Sun in Scorpio on the IC. She is in an environment where everyone "got on well, in harmony, no arguments," an idyllic scenario signified by Neptune in Libra in the third house. Within the home is someone who supports and cares for her, yet remains unseen. The invisibility of this person could reflect that there is something within Ann that supports and cares for her, an inner aspect of herself signified by the Sun on the IC.

Much of Ann's journey illustrates her chart elegantly. Ann loves to dance Spanish, fiery dancing and be the center of attention, and she loves the costume and pride of it, symbolized by Leo rising and Venus in Sagittarius in the fifth. She communes with the stars and is at one with the world and others, an idyllic state signified by Venus sextile Neptune.

Ann wishes to be happy, to have no regrets. We associate Venus with happiness, and Neptune in Libra, Venus' sign, will signify her longing for happiness. But the Venus sextile to Neptune brings the awareness that happiness may at times be elusive, while the square from Saturn to Venus signifies the possibility of later regrets. With a Venus Saturn square, it is easy to side with caution, failing to take risks which could result in happiness. Ann seems to recognize that she doesn't want to miss these opportunities, but just the thought of risk brings up an awareness of underlying danger. This is reflected in many areas of her chart. Besides the inherent caution of the Venus Saturn square, Ann has a developed, self-protective instinct, shown by the Sun in Scorpio on the IC, Pluto rising, and Mars in the first house. Ann is ever alert to threats to her well-being, and Mars and Pluto instantly alert her to any danger.

The most important aspect of this journey is the connection Ann makes to her hurt inner child. That this should happen on a Neptune journey with Neptune conjunct Mercury, a planet connected to childhood, seems appropriate. It's also a reminder that painful material can surface on any of the journeys, not only on journeys of planetary principles that are associated with difficulty.

JOE'S NEPTUNE JOURNEY

"It's a beautiful, hot summer's day. I'm lying on soft grass looking up at a cloudless sky, aware of all the smells and natural activity around me. Birds, flies, bees, breeze, etc.

"As I continue looking up at the sky, my body levitates towards the hot sun, and I am aware of passing through the transparent film. Hyperspacing between two different worlds, I feel myself entering a new atmosphere and new reality.

"My body feels weightless, and slowly I float down to earth and melt into the harmony of my natural surroundings. First of all, I feel flat, like a huge sheet covering the land and absorbing all the components of the natural landscape—all-conquering. (Neptune conjunct the MC)

"Suddenly, I am aware of a change in my physicality. I become small, light, about the size of a large insect. I jump around the plant life, playing with other insects, trampolining from the leaves of flowers. Exploring from my new perspective I feel no fear or danger because I am harmonious with everything around me.

"As I fly, jump, hop, play haphazardly, I feel very energized, and again I change my form. (Neptune in Sagittarius) I am like a mighty atom. A small, intense ball of energy. I am as quick as a bullet. (Sun in Aries trine Neptune)

"I take off and explore my new environment from a higher position, rising from the ground above the earth. The visual experience is like that of a camera on board a jet fighter traveling at tremendous speed over every variation in the earth's terrain. Over mountains, through forests, over oceans, under the earth, across valleys, etc., I am unstoppable. I experience every climatic change, too. Heat, cold, snow, rain, wind, and back to heat. (Sun Aries opposite Uranus, Neptune conjunct the MC)

"I can't really visualize an ideal, perfect world as such. But I am aware of an environment that is wholly natural, free of any notions of artificiality, synthetics, etc. No trace of other people, cars, buildings, aggression, noise, or pollution. I feel no danger in my world because I *am* my world and my world is me. (Neptune conjunct the MC)

"My wish is that this peace and harmony can last forever. As I leave my world, I feel forces pushing and pulling me like turbulence on an airplane. I return to the meadow through the lily pond, rising up through the water. The water dries on my back, and I return to the beautiful summer's day cleansed and refreshed and back into the arms of my smiling lover."

See page 31 for Joe's chart. Joe has Neptune closely conjunct the MC. Neptune is the most elevated planet in his chart, and at the beginning of the journey, Joe levitates into the sky. It is as if he is literally joining Neptune's elevated planetary position. He then floats down to earth, in touch with the harmony of his natural surroundings, giving expression to Neptune in Sagittarius. Once back down on the land, he covers it and absorbs it. We see here an expression of an all-encompassing Neptune on the MC, and the way the MC, via our experience of mother, eventually becomes our world.

A conflict within Joe between surrendering to feelings of oneness and needing to hold on to a sense of his separate self dominate his journey. After jumping around the plant life as a small insect, he becomes a mighty atom, a small, intense ball of energy, quick as a bullet, signified astrologically by the Sun in Aries opposite Uranus. This opposition is linked to Neptune, and it seems each times he surrenders to "mergy" feelings, which are essentially feminine, he is catapulted back into feelings that affirm his masculine identity.

Joe speaks of being all-conquering, which is essentially totally alien to Neptune's principle, and seems to be a defense against the "mergy" feelings

Neptune engenders. Joe is grappling to hold on to an ego, which the MC will generally signify. But in Joe's case, because he has both the Moon and Neptune on the MC, his sense of ego is swamped. He retreats to a part of himself where he has a sense of his separate identity, signified by his Sun in Aries. His fear of loss of self and of engulfment by a maternal object are defended against by manic, masculine activity.

Joe spends a large part of the journey looking down on the world rather than being a part of it, a defense against the harmony and the extent to which it threatens to swallow him up. He has a visual experience like that of a camera, achieving perspective and detachment, signified by the Sun in Aries opposite Uranus. When he feels secure within his separate identity, he can allow himself to dip in and out of the Neptunian realm.

Joe's travels over the body of the earth seem to incorporate sexual imagery in its mountains, valleys, forests, and oceans. The wide range of climatic changes he experiences suggests a wide emotional range and the possibility that he can "blow hot and cold" on an emotional level.

Joe feels no danger in his world because he *is* his world and his world is him, a beautiful illustration of being merged—symbolized by Neptune, with the world, symbolized by the MC. In this moment he is at peace, and his wish is for the feelings of peace to last forever. But even as he leaves, he feels forces pushing and pulling him like turbulence on an airplane. This must to relate to an inner turbulence that disturbs his feelings of inner peace.

He ends the journey rising up through the lily pond, as if he has been underwater; he has been submerged in the realm of the unconscious. He emerges feeling cleansed and refreshed, feelings that stay with him for some time afterwards, as if he had literally taken a dip in the sea, in Neptune's waters. Joe returns back to the arms of his smiling lover, perhaps the main context in which he experiences oneness, bliss, and fusion in his life.

Neptune was originally considered to be the god of clouds and rain, later becoming the god of fresh water and fertilizing water, and finally becoming what we understand Neptune to be today: the god of the sea. In his journey Joe seems to touch on all these aspects of Neptune.

Joe had some resistance to Neptune's realm, which we located within his chart, but he may also have been demonstrating a difficulty men in general have in allowing themselves to surrender to feelings of merging.

Both Ann's and Joe's guided imagery journeys had significance for them. Some participants find that imagining themselves in fairyland takes them back to the mythical stories of their childhood, and that stereotypic imagery then pervades their journey. If this happens for you, please don't just dismiss your journey. If you spend time talking your experience through with someone afterwards, you will find lots of personal significance in your images, cloaked by the trappings of mythic fairyland.

Most participants are left with a sense of wonder, whatever their actual images. Participants connect to a time when their imagination had a far greater range, when everyday reality did not impose its limits quite as strongly. This may reflect a longing for a time of innocence, when we all believed in fairies. This is what tipped Ann into her childhood memories.

This journey came to me in a dream, a most Neptunian way. I had been writing the Pluto journey the day before, which was still unfinished, so I had been thinking about guided imagery, but not about Neptune, and I awoke from a dream at 2 A.M. with this Neptune journey. I got up and wrote it down straight away. It was only later that I realized the transiting Sun was exactly on my Neptune. This is the only time this has ever happened to me.

CHAPTER 11

Pluto

Pluto is the third of the transpersonal planets, and it rules the transformation process: birth, death, and rebirth. We see this in nature in the compost heap, which starts out as waste vegetable matter that rots and decays, becoming rich and fertile compost. We see the same process in the caterpillar which turns into a chrysalis and, in turn, changes into a butterfly, and in the frog's spawn which hatches into tadpoles and metamorphose into frogs. Each change is irrevocable, each part of the process, inevitable and unstoppable. The old form dies, and the new is born out of the old, a process that results in a total transformation. Those with a strong Pluto in their chart (Pluto in hard aspect to a personal planet, the Ascendant, or MC) will be very much aware of the transformation process. Their life is marked by watersheds with a phase of life dying and a new phase beginning, the past being truncated and left behind.

Pluto is connected to an irrational, dark, feminine principle. Pluto's energy is nonverbal. It rules the reptilian brain, which governs our powerful, instinctive, yet primitive response to things. Pluto's principle is amoral, profound, deep, irreducible. It happens in the dark, invisibly; it is impossible to get hold of. Pluto is associated with deep unconscious processes. It has to do with things being taken underground for the purpose of being transformed. Pluto rules that which becomes buried and suppressed within the unconscious. Pluto also relates to buried treasure—in psychological terms, our instincts and unconscious.

Those of us with Pluto featured strongly in our chart have a susceptibility to suffer from periods of depression and despair. We may find life a struggle, and feel as if the cards are stacked against us and sink into feelings of hopelessness. These times are part of a natural cycle, and there will be times of renewal. Just as the compost heap takes time to transform the waste matter into sweet-smelling compost, so those of us with a strong Pluto need these apparently stagnant phases during which deep psychological changes occur. These may not be visible to others, but we will emerge from these dark times feeling that we have learned much that will stand us in good stead for the future.

Pluto is connected to power. Those with a strong Pluto often gravitate to positions of power. They may want to change society, to transform the world. If we try to take this power for ourselves rather than act as a channel for the energies of Pluto, then it will turn against us and destroy us. We are not the source of this power, but just an instrument of it. We are there to serve its cosmic purpose. We see this phenomenon in the lives of politicians who become identified with their power and believe it to be their own. This is the beginning of corruption and will provoke opposition very quickly. We witness politicians being cast aside, killed off, metaphorically, for a time, if not for good. We have to find ways of allowing the energies of Pluto to flow through us without becoming attached and identified with them.

Pluto is associated with the need to be in control. Those of us with a strong Pluto are often seen as very controlling. Fear underlies the need to be in control, fear of being vulnerable and in another's power. We are susceptible to power struggles with others who often find us domineering and dominating and feel they have to resist us at all costs. We may experience ourselves as powerless, as ineffectual, unable to influence outcomes that affect us. There can be a considerable gap between how we experience ourselves and how others experience us. Grasping this is the key to avoiding power struggles.

Pluto is connected to sex. During orgasmic sex the ego dies and we surrender ourselves to being joined, at one through another with something cosmic. The Victorians even called orgasm "the little death." It may feel intensely personal, but is ultimately beyond the personal. With the death of the ego, we transcend normal boundaries and meet on some other level.

Pluto is known as the higher octave of Mars, and it relates to the deeper will. It has to do with our obsessions, our compulsions. Those with a strong Pluto often have a strong personal magnetism, and some individuals can fall under their spell, while others may find them disquieting or unsettling. Either way, those with a strong Pluto can have a powerful impact on others and are generally thought of as charismatic.

Pluto is associated with paying our dues. It has to do with the rite of passage. As with the river Styx in the underworld, we have to pay the boatman. If we try to avoid these dues, a far higher price is exacted from us. Pluto demands that we pay tribute along the way, and there is retribution if this is denied. The gods take their revenge in a way which is inexplicably harsh in comparison to the misdeed. Pluto's placement will describe our psychic inheritance. The issues that remain unresolved in our bloodline are passed down from one generation to the next, sometimes skipping a generation. It then becomes the next generation's fate to try to redeem the situation. Sometimes our psychic inheritance is a far more extreme version of that which was left unresolved by the previous generations, but perhaps this is how fate ensures we grapple with it in our lifetime.

Pluto moves very slowly. Whole generations have Pluto in the same sign, and Pluto's sign will describe collective issues. As I write, Pluto has recently moved out of Scorpio. Throughout Pluto's ingress in Scorpio we had the realization of the impact and extent of sexual abuse and the advent of AIDS. Safe sex was a new concept, introducing a new code of behavior to sexual practice. Pluto's sign is primarily significant in terms of the collective issues we are born into.

The planets that Pluto aspects in our natal chart will show us which planetary principles are dragged underground and became unconscious, compulsive, and hence unfathomable and out of our control. For example, those with Sun Pluto will be mystified by the power struggles they find themselves caught up in, and will find that issues of empowerment dominate their lives.

There may again be an obvious wound in the father-child relationship, but its form is less easily defined. The father may have been a tyrant, abusive, threatening, intimidating, wielding power over the child. He may have been absent, leaving a black hole his presence should have filled. Or he may have been present and relatively mild, but emanated a psychological force, an emotional energy that in some subtle way dominated and controlled the atmosphere. Some with Sun Pluto aspects take years to begin to realize how their fathers wielded power over them and to understand how to free themselves from his control, even though he is no longer actually present. As adults, these people have an internalized image of the father, and it is this inner image that now dominates and controls them. They will attempt to redeem their experience of domination by the father through situations which recreate these dynamics. This is what Freud called the repetition compulsion, which is something we are all in the grip of with regard to our own particular issues. This is life's way of taking us forward, offering us an opportunity to bring unconscious and repressed material to consciousness and to heal ourselves.

The house Pluto occupies in our chart will describe the area of life we find most unfathomable—where we feel most fated. Pluto's house position describes an arena where we feel powerless, out of control, and yet strive to be powerful and in control. There is a struggle here to bring into consciousness, into the light, the impenetrable subterranean world of Pluto.

The guided imagery that follows presents various symbolic scenarios that will put us in touch with Pluto's principle, so that we may experience how this principle operates within us. Before you begin this journey please refer to *Some Guidelines Before Going on a Guided Imagery Journey* in Chapter 1 and go through the *Relaxation Exercise* given there.

Guided Imagery Journey on Pluto's Principle

— You are going down some old, worn stone steps, down, down, down, slowly, to some still, inky, blue-black water at the bottom of the steps.(short pause)

— Count the steps as you go down. (pause)

— When you get to the water, you go in and go beneath the surface and into its depths. (short pause)

— You are able to breathe underwater. (short pause)

— You go deeper and deeper and the water becomes blacker and blacker until you can see very little. (short pause)

— Your instinctual awareness becomes very strong. (short pause)

— You know you can sense what is around. (pause)

— Your shape is changing. (short pause)

— Allow yourself to change into a creature that is at home in this environment. (pause)

— Explore this underwater world that you now inhabit. (pause)

— Ahead are caves that have lain undisturbed under the water for millions of years. (short pause)

— At the entrance to a cave is a prehistoric creature. (short pause)

— What's the creature like? (pause)

— You are going to meet this creature and ask his or her permission to enter the cave. (short pause)

— The creature will ask something of you that you will not want to give as payment. (short pause)

— What does he or she ask of you? (pause)

— You must now agree to make this payment. (short pause)

— What is this like for you? (pause)

— You enter the cave and explore this subterranean world. (short pause)

— You are the first to enter for many thousands of years. (short pause)

— What do you find? (pause)

— Take your time as it's very dark and you have to explore through your instinctive sense of where things are. (long pause)

— You discover you have a knowledge of the depths that's been passed down to you through the generations going back into antiquity, and that you can draw on this knowledge for counsel. (pause)

— You find something of immense value to you in this cave. (short pause)

— What is it? (pause)

— You decide to leave and the creature guarding the entrance asks you to give up something further in order to leave the cave. (short pause)

— What is asked of you may not make sense to you, but you must satisfy the demand, whatever it is. (short pause)

— Hear what is asked, and agree to the payment. (pause)

— You leave the cave and now find you can see very easily in the deep, dark water. (short pause)

— You move through this world full of wonder. (long pause)

— Eventually, you begin to head up towards the surface. (pause)

— It's getting lighter and lighter, and you are changing back into your above-water shape. (short pause)

— You break the surface of the water and re-emerge, back in your usual body. (short pause)

— You climb back up the steps, counting them as you go up until you are back at the top again. (short pause)

When you are ready, open your eyes and slowly come back into the room.

Guidelines for How to Interpret Your Journey

Going down the old, worn stone steps can be likened to dropping beneath the surface of life down into our psychological depths. It is relevant here how many steps we choose to descend. Some will go down relatively few steps to reach the water while others will go down a great number. This may reflect how easily they can access unconscious material, or it may reflect how scary it is to descend into their unconscious depths.

The water is inky blue-black, as black is the color we associate with Pluto. We are going into a world where we are in touch with and rely on our instinctive awareness and knowledge. Going beneath the water is another way of taking us into our unconscious. In order that this is not a frightening experience, we are quickly told we can breathe underwater, and we change into a creature that is at home underwater. The creature we choose to become is often a graphic reflection of our natal Pluto. For instance, a man with Pluto rising in Leo opposite Mars, who saw himself as non-aggressive and yet frequently found himself in arguments that he claimed others instigated, changed into a great white shark, one of the most ferocious fish. He claimed this was simply for defensive purposes; no one messes with a great white shark. But after going on this journey, he had a glimmering of understanding that he might have more of a part to play in his clashes than he'd realized.

Some participants have some vivid and enjoyable experiences exploring the underwater world which is Pluto's realm. The caves are symbolic of our ancestral lineage. What we find in them is always of immense significance, and represents the buried riches that Pluto symbolizes, the wisdom of our instinctive knowledge and intuitive awareness that frequently remains unconscious.

The kind of prehistoric creature we imagine guarding the cave entrance will reflect our Pluto's placement. How frightening or approachable the figure is may reflect our feelings about the things that lie in our unconscious. We are asked to pay something, which is about paying our dues. It is our rite of passage. What we have to pay may surprise us. It is often a high price, but will always have relevance and importance to us. No one seems to get off lightly, and it may take some time for us to talk through and unravel the meaning of what we are asked to relinquish. One women was asked to give up her eyes. She was shocked, but agreed to it. When we talked it through afterwards, it was clear she needed to stop "looking outwards" and begin to "look inwards" more. She lost her sight to gain insight.

How willing or resistant we are to pay what is being asked is also relevant. On the one hand, being willing to pay may indicate an openness in us and a willingness to change, but I have seen an appropriate resistance in some participants and an ability to renegotiate the terms. When participants openly rebel or cheat at this stage, I do not feel it bodes well for them. If this is a metaphor for paying our dues in life, those who cheat usually get their comeuppance, and when it's Pluto we try to cheat, it is usually a harsh one. We are not dealing here with ordinary morality, but with something of a far different order, and I would want to explore with those who cheat at this stage what dangers might lie ahead.

Once in the cave, participants explore a terrain that can be seen to represent, metaphorically, their unconscious. Many will discover jewels, a classic symbol of the "buried treasure," representing the riches lying dormant in their unconscious mind. Others discover more obscure things. In order to understand the symbolism, the participant will need to talk things through afterwards. One participant discovered piles of old bones, almost as if a massacre had taken place, and related this to all her buried rage. Sometimes the meaning is still not at all clear, even after talking it through, in which case it needs to be left. The symbolism will become clear over time, and the participant may not yet be ready to know consciously something that they do know on another level. At times, too, we may think we have understood the symbolism of images only to discover much later a whole new level of understanding, truths we were not yet ready to confront, that it was not appropriate we confront.

The cave is dark as an incentive to participants to "see" and feel their way around the interior of the cave instinctually. They are encouraged to recognize and trust their instinctual knowledge as something that can be relied upon, that they have within a deep, innate wisdom. The pervasive feeling of antiquity helps participants to get a sense of their place in their ancestral lineage.

Another payment is asked in order to leave the cave. For some, this payment connects back to the first payment and is in some way an extension of it, often illuminating further what needs to be relinquished or changed in the life at the current time. For others, this payment is connected to what they have just discovered, which may mean it has to remain in the unconscious realm and is not to be brought back up into consciousness at this point.

Usually by now, participants are relaxed and at ease in this underwater world. The next part is a time in which they can enjoy the benefits of having dipped down into Pluto's realm. This may be a particularly beautiful part of the imagery with brilliant fish appearing.

As with out-of-body experiences, it is important that once participants have surfaced, they are back in their own body, and that they climb back up the same number of steps that they descended. We do not want to leave participants not fully back on the surface of their life, as it were.

Other People's Journeys

Let's go on to look at the charts and journeys of a woman and man who did this journey on October 2, 1993 and June 10, 1996, respectively. The accounts are reproduced here verbatim, as they were recorded at the time. Where I have made connections back to their natal chart, I have inserted the astrological signifiers in parentheses in the text.

OLIVIA'S PLUTO JOURNEY

"I went down the stairs, 110 steps. It felt cold and damp going down, but the nearer I got to the water the warmer and warmer it was. When I got to the pool, it was steamy and warm like a Jacuzzi, and inky dark. It felt very comforting going into it and being underneath— warm and fluid. I swam downwards.

"When I got down to the bottom, the first sense that came to me was danger. I wanted to change into being my cat, or at least to have him very close, but I knew he couldn't live in this environment, and I desperately wanted him with me. I became an eel and then a sponge— but I became waterlogged and couldn't move. So eventually I became a mermaid so I could swim and move around. (emphasis in Sagittarius and the ninth house, Neptune conjunct the MC)

"I found a beautiful, smooth, round stone that turned into an enormous pearl, and when I held it, the feeling of danger went. I knew that all would be well while it was with me—I hung it around my neck. (Venus in Scorpio square Pluto)

"When I got to the cave, the prehistoric monster looked horrific—like tripe—with tentacles on his head. He was holding his arms across the doors which were bulging, as if about to burst open. (Pluto in the eighth sesquiquadrate Jupiter)

"I asked him if I could go in. He said yes, but in return he wanted my soul. I said no, that my soul was mine and he couldn't have it. So he said he'd take my spirit. I asked him exactly why he wanted them and he said he wanted to keep a bit of me so I would return. I said that if he let me in, when I came out I would give him my pearl, as I knew the pearl was protective and beautiful and that I would return many times to see it because it felt a part of me. He agreed. (Sun trine Pluto, Venus square Pluto)

"With this, the door stopped bulging and he opened it and let me in. It was even darker. I went in and I found beautiful, black oysters with lovely, black pearls. They felt very precious and very beautiful. (Venus in Scorpio square Pluto)

"My mother was there with a baby—holding it in her arms and looking at it. I sensed a poignancy and simplicity that overwhelmed me. I wanted to go near and hold them both, but for a moment I just needed to watch, as it was a special moment and my joining them would have felt invasive and broken the spell. They were totally enraptured with each other. I held my arms out and sent them love, but I was sad, as I felt like an outsider and desperately wanted to be part of it. (Venus in Scorpio square Pluto in the eighth)

"On the floor was a bucket full of anemones, masses of them. I bent down to look further, and I saw that the bucket was bleeding. The blood was bright red, pulsating and warm. I tasted it, and it was like nectar, smooth and sweet. It was flowing all over the floor. (Venus in Scorpio square Pluto in the eighth)

"I bathed in the blood and felt really connected to the pearls, my mother, and the anemones, as the blood flowed between them all and me. I was dabbling around, laughing with pleasure, and I was overwhelmed with a wonderful, very strong, full feeling inside. (Pluto in the eighth)

"I must have fallen asleep in the blood because suddenly I realized it was time to get back. I panicked and started running, and then my mother noticed me and came running to me with the baby, and held and kissed me. I started crying as I said I had to leave, and I pleaded for her to come with me. I just couldn't leave her now that I'd found her. But she said, 'No,' and led me further back into the cave and said, 'This is what you were meant to find—they are a part of me.' (Venus in Scorpio in the tenth square Pluto in the eighth)

"She handed me a box with the most exquisitely beautiful jewels—sapphires, diamonds, rubies, emeralds. The colors were so rich—masses of them. I asked her what I should do with them. She said each time I came down to visit I could take one of them back with me, and look at it and wear it. And when I felt I knew every part of it, I could return for another bit. I kissed her and chose a black pearl, and kissed her again and left. I returned and gave the creature my white pearl, and then ran all the way up the stairs." (Sun trine Pluto, Venus in Scorpio square Pluto in the eighth)

See page 34 for Olivia's chart. Olivia descends 110 steps, which may reflect her fear of dipping down into her unconscious. It may also reflect the gap between her conscious and unconscious sides. The steamy water is an indication of her passionate nature.

Olivia is initially afraid, wanting her cat near her. He has somehow come to represent safety to her. She goes on to find a stone, which transforms into a pearl, acting as a talisman for her throughout the journey. She invests it with the power to protect her from danger. Her pearl can be seen to represent wisdom. We speak of "pearls before swine" when we have wasted words of wisdom on someone who is unappreciative. So, perhaps what Olivia has found to protect herself is her wisdom. There is a link back to her cat here. Her cat carries a projection of her unconscious feminine wisdom, which brings us back to the astrology. The sign associated with big cats is Leo, and Olivia has Pluto, the planet associated with unconscious feminine wisdom, in Leo.

Olivia first changes into an eel, which, aside from the phallic symbolism, is apt, as eels travel thousands of miles in the course of their lives. Olivia has an emphasis in Sagittarius, a stellium in the ninth house, as well as Jupiter in the third, all associated with long journeys in various ways. She then becomes a sponge, which is perhaps a metaphor for the potential of Neptune on the MC to be psychologically absorbent. Olivia settles on being a mermaid, a mythic creature, and retains much of her human form. This reflects both her Neptune on the MC and Venus square Pluto. Mermaids are associated with sexuality and seduction.

The prehistoric creature becomes a threatening and ominous monster for Olivia, maybe mirroring her fear and hostility. She is able to negotiate with him, a Libran predilection. Perhaps this reflects her ability to dialogue with disassociated parts of herself. She manages to get a very good deal. She only has to pay once when she leaves, so in effect she gets in for nothing, and she keeps the best pearl for herself. She strikes this deal by getting to know the monster, by using her Libran relating skills, and ascertaining what he really wanted. This was a continuing relationship, which we could interpret as a continuing relationship between Olivia and her inner monster.

On entering the cave, Olivia finds black pearls, which she recognizes as very precious and beautiful. Black is a color we associate with Pluto and the unconscious. The black pearls represent a rare wisdom, the wisdom of the unconscious.

Perhaps the white pearl represents what Olivia knows consciously; she is giving up what she knows consciously, trusting it will return to her because it is in fact a part of her that she can claim back at any time. This seems to reflect the workings of memory. Experiences are stored in the conscious mind for a time, but then slip into the unconscious. We "forget," but we can in fact access these things again. They are not truly lost to us, but simply slip beneath our conscious memory. We have all had the experience of rediscovering what we have always known. This is very much Pluto's domain.

Olivia sees her mother with a baby. This seems to be an early childhood memory, either of herself with her mother or of her mother with a sibling. She witnesses the special bond between her mother and the baby. There is something very primordial and primitive about Olivia's journey. She seems to be in touch with aspects of her birth. The anemones may represent nipples, as they have a pronounced center. The bucket, a container, is bleeding. This is surely a symbolic representation of the womb, yet when Olivia tastes the blood, it tastes of nectar, smooth and sweet. So it seems the bucket is a representation of the breast, and there is an abundance of breast milk; the milk is flowing all over the floor. Birth and the matrilineal line are both parts of Pluto's domain.

Olivia finds her mother, and the deep bond that exists between them, but is then in grief that she has to leave. Olivia has to separate from her mother to become an individual and adult in her own right. Before Olivia leaves, her mother takes her to where the most exquisitely beautiful jewels are, right in the depths of the cave. It seems Olivia has inherited her femininity and sexuality from her mother. This is a precious inheritance to do with regeneration and creativity. Olivia's journey is about birth, separation, and the gift of life.

RORY'S PLUTO JOURNEY

"I went down six steps, similar to those from a river embankment. I didn't notice the other immediate surroundings. I seemed to carry on, down into the water, on solid ground. (Pluto in Virgo)

"Eventually, the ground was no more, and I was floating downward. (Pluto in the twelfth house) I started to breathe through my arms, the skin on my arms acting like gills, twitching as they absorbed and expelled oxygen. I metamorphosed into a stout little fish with big lips, about the size of a very plump salmon but not salmon shaped.

"I couldn't sense much from the gloom of the deep water. It was murky, maybe some mossy seaweeds growing upwards here and there. I didn't see any other creatures, but felt I was being watched by them. Small, yellow eyes piercing the gloom. (Pluto in the twelfth house)

"Eventually, I came across some caves. Almost designed. Three openings next to each other, perfectly similar in every way. They were set a little higher than where I was swimming. (Mercury in the eleventh house) Beyond the cave entrances it looked very dark. As I go to enter, a creature with a face and neck like a Tyrannosaurus makes itself visible. Its grisly mouth opens, revealing hundreds of sharp, white teeth. The shape of the jaw when opened has a morbid, smilelike shape. (Saturn opposite Pluto) I have nothing for the creature by way of toll, so I swim through a smaller hole off to the side where there are numerous other entrances. I don't feel guilty for avoiding the creature or fear my capture. (Moon opposite Jupiter) I know that it will stay guarding the main entrance. (Pluto in the twelfth house)

"Once in the cave, I immediately find an area basked in light from massive chimneylike structures that reach up to the surface. Coral grows like a majestic underworld forest. (Sun Pluto conjunction in the twelfth house) I soon realize that this cannot be, though. It is something imagined. (Mercury square Neptune) There is no such light penetrating at this depth. I feel very lost in this world. I feel even less sure about the cave than anywhere. (Sun Pluto conjunction in the twelfth)

"I find a room within the cave that is like a cathedral (Moon opposite Jupiter) carved from stone. Again, I struggle to see details through the gloom. (Sun Pluto conjunction in the twelfth) I am then aware of some kind of inherited knowledge. This leads me along a clearly laid trail of lovely round stones, carefully laid out. The terrain is quite earthly, like a mountainous, cliffy area, with no vegetation. (Sun Pluto conjunction in Virgo)

"I am led by the trail to yet another area of the cave which seems the darkest and the vastest. (Sun Pluto conjunction in the twelfth) Shining out to me is a script, fairly thick and typed. It is my script. Every idea, every story strand, every character that I have ever invented in a script is included. It has my name on the front. I know this script will make my fortune. People will be enthusing about it across the world. It will be dramatized, serialized, made for film, adapted for radio. It represents my every success. It is all of my creativity honed into one piece of work. (Sun Uranus Pluto conjunction in the twelfth, Sun quintile Jupiter, Jupiter in Gemini conjunct the MC)

"I swim off and have forgotten about the guard who looms up, surprising me. (Moon opposite Jupiter) I have been cornered by it this time. I expected it to ask me how I got in, but it didn't. Instead, it was demanding an exit toll, apparently oblivious to my means of entry. I felt I had no option but to give it one of my gills. (Moon trine Mercury, Mercury sextile Jupiter) This was ripped off and left me in quite a lot of discomfort and unable to breathe properly.

"It is easier to move through the water now, and lighter, as my eyes have adjusted. A lovely, greeny-yellow color is created by the combination of the water, light, and vegetation. The world feels less hostile than it did, but I still sense that the creatures of this world are hiding from me, their eyes piercing the darker areas like little yellow lights. (Sun Pluto conjunction in the twelfth) I am keen to get back to the surface, especially with my missing gill and the subsequent drowsiness and lack of breath it is causing me. I rise towards the surface quickly.

"Reaching for the bright blue light above me, I quickly metamorphose to human form. As I climb the six steps, I notice the pool is surrounded by sheer cliffs that reach up into the night. The texture of the rock is very pronounced, slightly furrowed like an old oak tree trunk. (Sun Pluto conjunction in Virgo in the twelfth) The whole scene is very striking and feels as if it is lit by a very low full moon. I am pleased to be back on solid ground. Deep water always puts fear into me."

See page 35 for Rory's chart. Rory descends six steps to reach the water. He does not have to descend far to reach unconscious material. As he descends under water, he is still on solid ground. He is familiar with things that lie just beneath the surface. We see here the familiarity with the unconscious that we might expect in someone with a Sun Pluto conjunction in the twelfth house.

Rory uses his arms as gills. Mercury is associated with the arms and the lungs and is the ruler of Virgo, the sign Rory's Sun and Pluto fall in. The plump fish is obviously well-fed, signified by the Moon Jupiter opposition, which links harmoniously with Mercury.

Rory cannot see much in the gloom of the deep water. It is murky, and there are mossy seaweeds here and there. He has entered a deeper level of the unconscious, psychological territory that he is unfamiliar with, ill-defined and threatening. He senses creatures that he cannot see are watching him. This sixth sense is likely to be well developed in Rory, with the Sun, Uranus, and Pluto in the twelfth house. His intuition is likely to be something he can rely on to protect him from danger, but it could have a paranoid inclination. This may relate back to an earlier time when invisible danger did lurk and threatened him, which Pluto in the twelfth can signify.

The creature he meets at the entrance to the cave has a grisly mouth, hundreds of sharp, white teeth, and a macabre smile. It may represent Rory's fears of being consumed by past history or past hurt. It could also indicate his own unconscious aggression; this creature represents an aspect of himself.

Rory cheats and gets into the cave by a different entrance. At the time, he believes there will be no payback. Yet later, when he leaves the cave feeling open and less defended, he gets caught and has to pay to leave. While he got away with only paying once, this evasive dynamic has its own less visible price. It requires that Rory remain in his more suspicious, paranoid side, ever alert to danger. When he lets down his guard and becomes more open, he inevitably gets caught. We can see this signified in his chart. Moon in Sagittarius opposite Jupiter describes Rory's open, trusting, expansive side which can become careless, while the Sun conjunct Pluto opposite Saturn is more mistrustful, self-protective, and defensive. It may seem that when Rory lets go with his enthusiastic side, he gets clobbered by harsh reality. But in effect he has set this up for himself.

Rory has to give up one of his gills and is hampered in his ability to breathe and move through the water. Gills are associated with Mercury, which is linked to the Moon Jupiter opposition in Rory's chart, and which rules his Sun Pluto conjunction. The price Rory pays has direct links to these dynamics within his chart.

The cave Rory enters is all lit up. He finds coral growing like a majestic underworld forest. Uranus is known as the bringer of light. Here, it is conjunct the Sun and Pluto in the twelfth house. Briefly, light shines on his deepest unconscious feelings. But then he realizes this is impossible, that no light can penetrate at this depth. Rory says he feels very lost in this world, the world of the unconscious. He may feel lost because he has lost touch with his feelings of loss, which swirl around in an ill-defined way in his unconscious.

Rory finds a room that is like a cathedral. This must be signified by Jupiter, the planet associated with religion. This is perhaps Rory's attempt to find a place of safety. A cathedral is a sanctuary, but it is also rather grandiose. Perhaps when Rory has difficulties he retreats into a grandiose part of himself.

Rory finds a trail to the darkest and vastest cave, where he finds his script. This script is inside him, reflecting his capabilities. The trail to his script is laid out. He is led there, which implies that his path in life is laid out for him, that he feels he is fated. He finds his script when in the darkest, vastest part of the unconscious. His creativity emerges from the unconscious depths of his psyche. This is a beautiful illustration of the Sun conjunct Pluto in the twelfth house.

Rory desires recognition, fame, wealth, and to communicate with everyone. Rory's ambitions are huge. We see Jupiter in Gemini on the MC in his desire to communicate globally. We also see the Sun, Uranus, and Pluto in the twelfth house opposite Saturn in his desire for worldwide fame and recognition. With the Sun in the twelfth, there is a propensity to feel overlooked. Rory's aspirations may partly be to compensate for this. This is especially likely when the Sun is linked to Saturn and Pluto.

When Rory leaves, he has to pay a price. Perhaps having found something precious, he can now afford to pay his dues. The world is less hostile and threatening, but he is still alert to danger, to the eyes piercing the darker areas like little yellow lights. He is still keen to get back to the surface. He is not comfortable in this terrain, the world of his unconscious. Even when he surfaces, the pool is surrounded by sheer cliffs, perhaps a reflection of how impossible he feels his ambitions to be, how hard it will be to climb to the top and realize them. He ends his journey saying deep water always puts fear into him. Although his unconscious material is not far away, it is nevertheless threatening. Rory demonstrates on his journey that if you want a full, happy, and conscious life, there is no avoiding the pain. If he is to realize his creative potential, he has to go to where the demons lie.

These two journeys are both powerful illustrations of the deep, inner wisdom and instinctual knowledge that lie in the depths of our unconscious. Accessing it may be painful, but we risk living a stunted life if we choose to ignore it. Once we learn to negotiate the depths, we can dip down there for our jewels, as Olivia does, any time we want.

Afterthoughts

All the participants who went on the various journeys presented in this book found their experiences helpful. Lance said it was enlightening, and Rory was thrilled to have found his script. Ann claims it changed her life, that it stirred up a lot of buried memories and feelings that took her into counseling. She made internal changes, and now, three years later, external change has followed.

The date each participant went on their guided imagery journey is included so that those of you who are astrologers, can, if you want to, see the transits and progressions participants were experiencing at the time of their journeys. Those of you who are familiar with astrology will no doubt hear the participants speak their transits as well as their charts. In-depth discussion of transits and progressions was beyond the scope of this book but is nevertheless a very exciting part of working in this way.

My commentary on the journeys is not a definitive interpretation by any means. There are always plenty of other ways journeys can be understood and new levels of meaning can surface over time. My interpretation does not always tally with the participant's understanding, and this does not have to mean that one of us is right and the other wrong. We can both be right. A participant's understanding of their own journey has to be right, but it is limited by what they are able to take on board at the time. My commentaries are primarily a guide to help you think about your own journeys.

When I am working individually with a client who has been on a guided imagery journey, I help them to make connections between the content of their imagery and their life, both their current situation and their early life. This integrates the meaning of the journey into their current life; it grounds their experience. This is a further step that you can take, with a friend, counselor, or therapist. However, these journeys contain different levels of meaning which coexist simultaneously. If we attribute our imagery too concretely to things that are currently occurring in our life, we can limit our wider understanding. We can miss a whole dimension of what is being revealed.

We understand the content of our guided imagery journey at the level we are capable of at the time. This is a built-in safety net. This is also why it can be helpful to keep a record of our imagery. We can go back, sometimes several years later, and see things we were unable to see at the time, things that perhaps threatened our idea of ourselves or were too painful. Several years later, when we have worked through a particular issue, we can see how it was metaphorically knocking on the door of our conscious mind. Recognizing our past capacity to be in denial may enable us to be more open to acknowledging certain aspects of ourselves in the present. With hindsight, we see both the benefit of being less defended and the defensive mechanisms still at work within us.

These guided imagery journeys on the planetary principles are based on my understanding and experience of these principles—and my orientation is a reflection of me. I hope this book has deepened your understanding of the symbolic and helps you on your journey of self-discovery.

Related Books from The Crossing Press

HEALING WITH ASTROLOGY

by Marcia Starck

Medicine Woman and medical astrologer Marcia Starck provides detailed descriptions of the correspondence between the planetary cycles and a variety of healing systems—vitamin therapy, herbs, music, color, crystals, gemstones, flower remedies, aromatherapy, and unification rituals, and offers us the opportunity to reunite the healing wisdom of the Goddess tradition with the planets and stars as they appear in our birth charts.

$14.95 • Paper • ISBN 0-89594-862-1

AN ASTROLOGICAL HERBAL FOR WOMEN

By Elisabeth Brooke

An extensive guide to the use of herbs in healing the mind, body and spirit, organized by planetary influence. Includes the astrological significance of 38 common herbs, as well as their physical, emotional, and ritual uses.

$12.95 • Paper • ISBN 0-89594-740-41

SOUL-CENTERED ASTROLOGY: A KEY TO YOUR EXPANDING SELF

By Alan Oken

From the best selling author of *Alan Oken's Complete Astrology*, a dynamic new way to interpret the horoscope—the first to reveal the soul's path to inner enlightenment and outer fulfillment.

$1895 • Paper • ISBN 0-89594-811-7

POCKET GUIDE TO ASTROLOGY

By Alan Oken

$6.95 • Paper • ISBN 0-89594-820-6

To receive a current catalog from The Crossing Press,
please call toll-free, 800-777-1048.
Visit our Website on the Internet at: www.crossingpress.com